W9-ASN-902

Better Homes and Gardens®

celebrate the SEASON®

contents

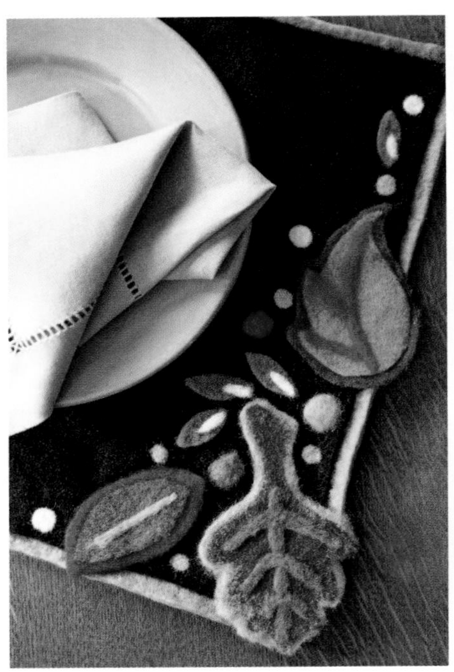

gifts

122 USE YOUR TALENTS to surprise everyone on your gift list. From delicious food gifts whipped up in the kitchen to fun and festive decorations created out of love, you'll be rewarded by smiles and heartfelt appreciation.

kids

138 FOR ALL AGES of kids, from preschool through graduation, here are fun projects designed for a variety of skill levels. From finger-printing to making accessories for a tea party, kids will be inspired to experience and show their artistic side!

in a twinkling

A FUN COLLECTION of holiday projects that are easy on time yet leave a lasting, super-festive impression.

Printed in the United States of America.
ISSN: 10980733 ISBN: 978-0-696-30217-6

it's show time

There's something absolutely magical about Christmas. As December 25 draws near, I revel at the sight of snow. To me, those billowy flakes are a sign that the most glorious season of the year has arrived.

It's a greatly anticipated time when I kick my diet to the curb and enjoy all the goodness that comes with the season. I love to try new recipes and share them with all the people that bring me happiness all year long. Whether I serve food for a holiday gathering or give food to neighbors in homemade wraps, it's immensely rewarding to share delicious treats that come from my very own kitchen.

And the decorating! For me, it's so enjoyable to turn our home into a fabulous wintry wonderland for family and friends. New trims, welcoming tabletops, updated color schemes—I feel like Santa having long-awaited fun.

Yes, the holiday season lifts spirits and encourages creative giving. Yet often ideas run short, as does time. That's where *Better Homes and Gardens® Celebrate the Season* steps in.

Celebrate the Season is your personal on-call idea bank that offers oodles of ideas for holiday menus, crafts, decorations, gifts—whatever it takes to make the season bright, memorable, and enjoyable.

Whether your style is traditional, contemporary, whimsical, or eclectic, in this book you'll find dozens of ideas to blend into your own wintry wonderland. Discover delicious new recipes—tasty appetizers, decadent desserts, and everything in between. Count on gift giving to be more meaningful than ever with make-it-yourself projects to surprise and delight family and friends.

Christmas is a magical time of year. And with the help of *Celebrate the Season*, you become the magician.

Enjoy the season,

Sue Banker

fall

COLOR-DRENCHED INSPIRATION

CHANGE THINGS UP

As summer transitions to autumn and the decorating palette turns to one inspired by Mother Nature, the projects in this chapter usher in welcome changes.

Falling for Felt

Master the art of wool felting. These warmly textured decorating accents and lapel pins display your creativity.

Artful Coasters

Small felt squares, used as coasters, act as mini artist canvases.

WHAT YOU NEED

Ruler
Scissors
Tracing paper; pencil
Wool felt in white, black, and accent colors
Felting needle tool
Felting brush pad

WHAT YOU DO

1. For each coaster, cut a 3¾-inch square from white wool felt.
2. Trace the patterns on page 153. Use the patterns to cut flowers and stems from wool felt. For stems, cut ¼×12-inch strips, cutting to lengths as needed.
3. Felt the white square on the black around the edges as shown in Photo A, following needle punch manufacturer's instructions. Trim a narrow border as shown in Photo B.
4. Using patterns as a guide, draw the stem on white felt. Felt the stem in place as shown in Photos C and D. Felt remaining pieces in place as shown in Photos E and F. Felt all pieces in place until the surface is level enough to support a glass.

Falling Leaves Mat

Edge a table mat with stylized leaves. For each mat, cut an 11-inch square from black wool felt. Felt it to a 12-inch square of teal wool felt. Trace the patterns on page 154. Use the patterns to cut pieces from wool felt. Felt the leaf pieces together first, then felt them to the mat. Using the photo and patterns as a guide, felt all leaf and berry shapes to the mat.

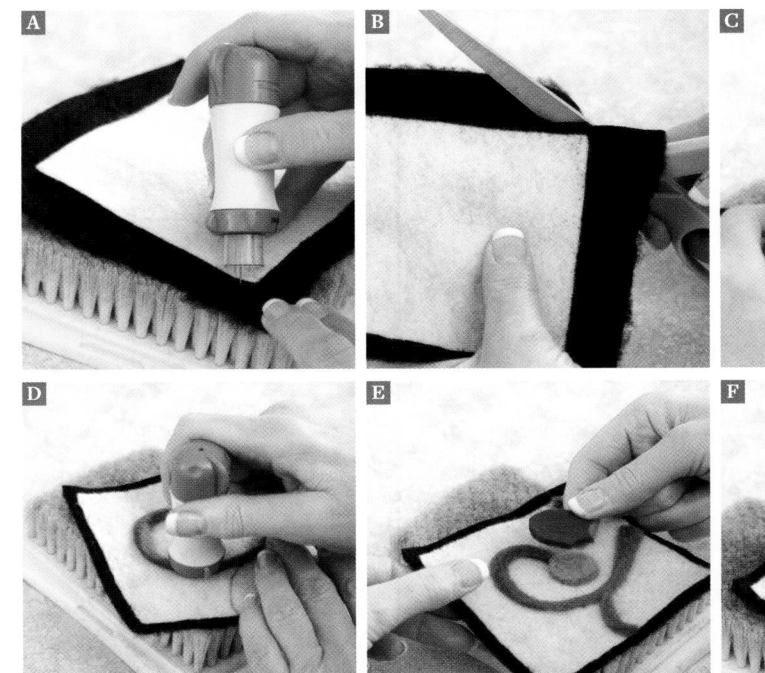

Art Deco Bowl

Dare to be dimensional. Create a colorful felted bowl to hold a bouquet of pinecones.

WHAT YOU NEED

Ruler
Scissors
Tracing paper; pencil
Wool felt in desired colors
Felting needle tool
Felting brush pad

WHAT YOU DO

1. Trace the patterns on page 152. Use the patterns to cut pieces from felt.

2. Using the photo and pattern as a guide, felt details onto shapes, then felt the shapes to bowl sides, setting aside corner pieces. Cut ½-inch-wide strips from black to line each of the four sides. Position so that the black edge shows slightly from the right side; felt in place.

3. For each corner, cut a ½×2-inch inside corner piece. Overlap the corner piece ¼ inch on one corner and felt in place as shown in Photos A and B. Shape the corner and felt the remainder of the corner piece in place to secure the corner as shown in Photos C and D.

4. For each corner, felt the dots to the outside corner pieces as shown in Photo E. Place a dotted piece at corner along seam; felt in place as shown in Photo F.

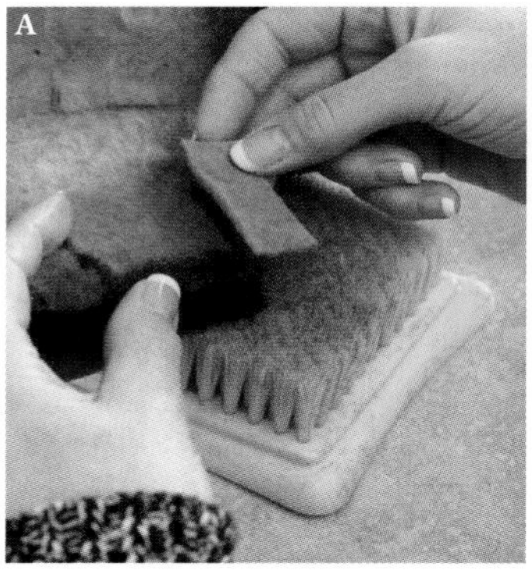

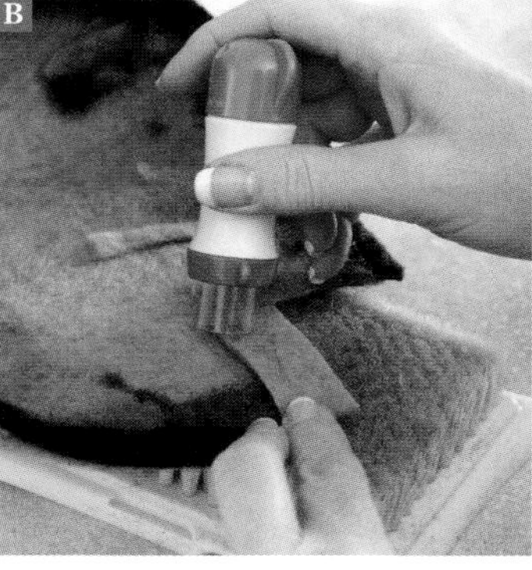

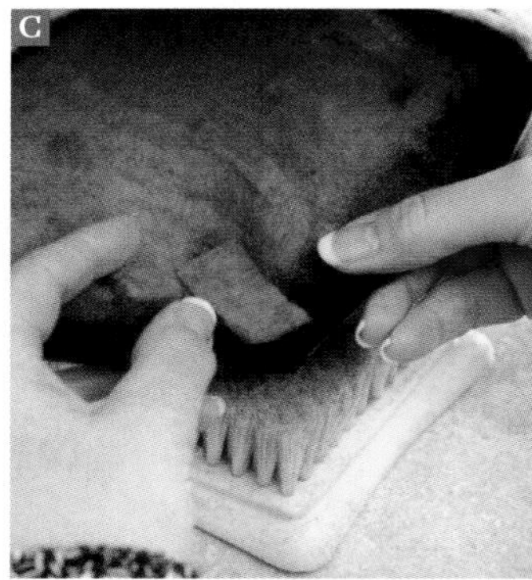

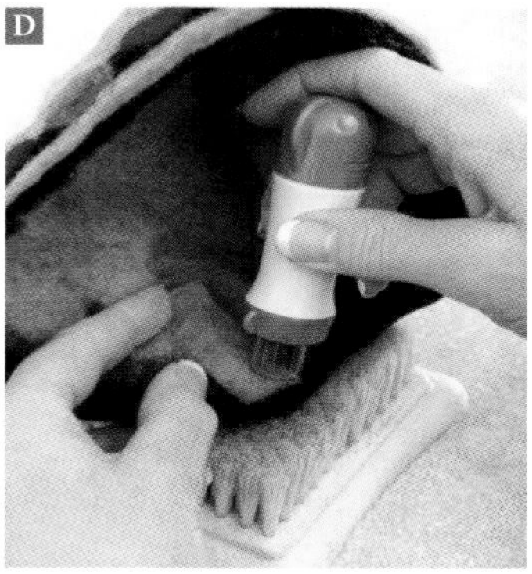

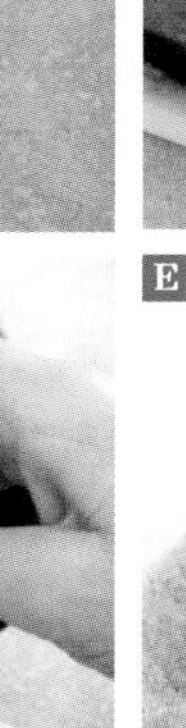

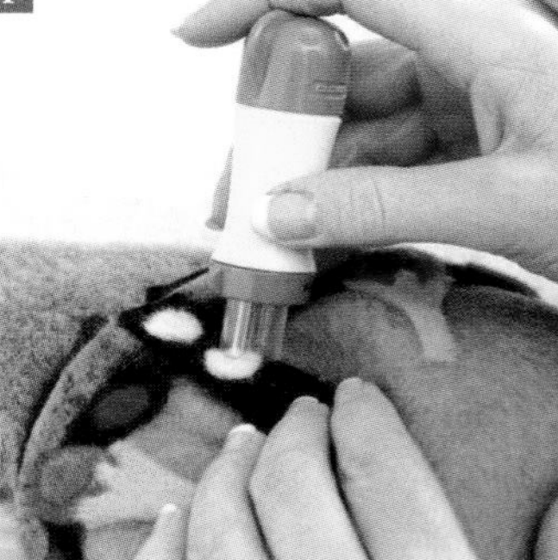

Cute as a Button

Button brads, available with scrapbooking supplies, decorate pretty lapel pins. Cut two or three larger circles from wool , felt together following the instructions from the felting needle manufacturer, and poke a hole in the center with an awl. Insert the brad prongs through the hole and secure on the back. To attach to a lapel, stitch a pin from jewelry finding to the back.

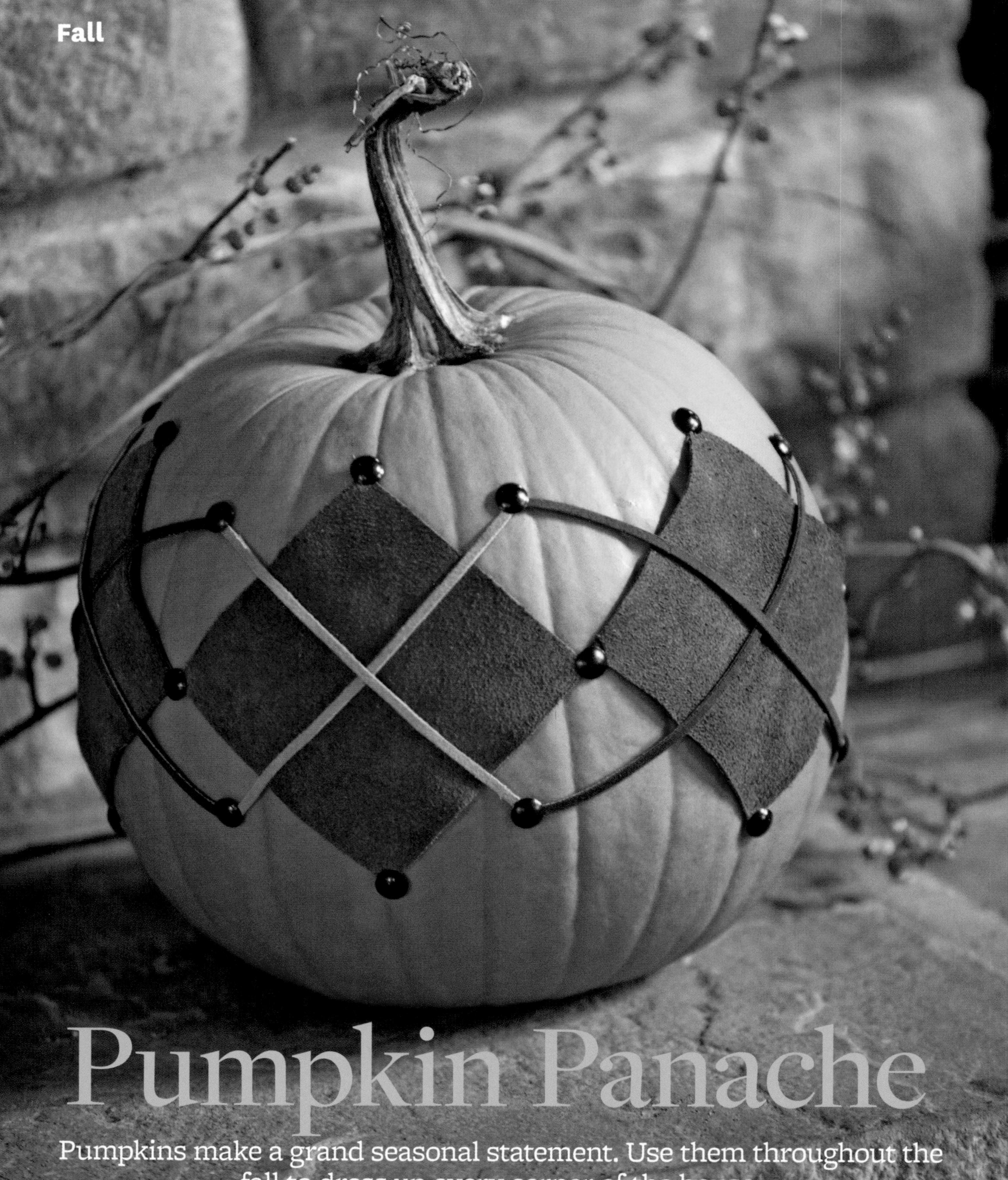

Pumpkin Panache

Pumpkins make a grand seasonal statement. Use them throughout the fall to dress up every corner of the house.

Argyle Band

What a fun, easy pattern. Cut squares from suede to tack on point using upholstery tacks. Use an awl to make a pair of holes between each diamond as shown in photo. Poke ends of leather lacing into holes to form an X extending beyond each suede square and secure with upholstery tacks. Drilled pumpkins last for a few days; use artificial ones for longer displays.

In Stitches

These little wonders appear as though they have been hand-stitched. To get the look, first secure a length of suede lacing around the center. Then randomly poke holes randomly above and below center to insert different colors of lacing. Angles and varying lengths have the effect of freehand stitching.

Color Burst

Suede lacing gently defines pumpkin creases. Drill holes in creases from stem to varying lengths. Cut suede lacing ½ inch longer than each punched length. Use an awl to secure lacing in holes.

Stylized Wheat

With long straight stems and V-shape branches, this primitive wheat design in brown and rust is elegant yet simple.

Pattern Play

Even miniature pumpkins join in the fun. Use an awl to make holes, then add leather lacing and, if desired, upholstery tacks. Freehand designs or use a ruler to guide marks. Follow Photos A through D for steps to make the laced shapes.

For the Family

Personalize your pumpkin with a bold initial "stitched" front and center. Using the photo as a guide, mark three concentric circles (one at a time) on pumpkin. Use lids, plates, and bowls as guides and poke approximately every inch, using a pen as shown in Photo A. Drill holes where marked as shown in Photo B. Using an awl, poke one end of suede lacing into one of the holes. Work around the circle, poking lace into the next hole as shown in Photo C to complete the circle. Mark, drill, and lace two larger circles. Draw a letter in the center of the circle, drill holes to outline, then fill in with suede lacing.

Nice and Natural

Keep it simple with easy decorating projects that subtly welcome autumn.

Walnut Photo Holder

Give nature photos, family pics, or place cards a seasonal lift. Drill a small hole in the top of a walnut. (Choose nuts with flat bottoms to stand.) Cut a 6-inch length of 18-gauge wire. Wrap one end of the wire twice around a wide marking pen. Remove the pen, then pinch the loops flat. Insert the opposite end into the nut. Slip a photo or card between the loops.

Stones, No Sticks

Polished from a crafts store or picked up along the shore, stones go hand-in-hand with rustic wood frames. Arrange stones on a frame, then use strong quick-set glue to adhere them permanently in place.

Go Nuts

Add fall flavor to a tabletop or mantel with cylinder vases filled with a variety of nuts and wheat. Roll coordinating scrapbook paper into decorative cuffs that slip inside the vase. Displaying a pair, side by side, makes a bold statement when space allows. Place dried leaves and a couple of nuts alongside the vases to complete the arrangement.

Gourd-eous

The natural beauty of gourds—shape, color, and texture—shines through as seasonal showstoppers.

Easy Peasy

Cut off the top of a pumpkin, then scoop out the flesh. Place a pillar candle in the center, with blocks of wet floral foam surrounding it. Poke short-cut flowers and berries into the foam.

Winning Combination

A swan gourd fresh from the vine stands in for a vase in this autumn arrangement. To prep the gourd, cut off the stem end with a sharp knife. Use an apple corer or a small pumpkin carving tool to hollow out the top few inches of the neck. Insert fall foliage—such as oak at its peak color. No water required.

Clever Carving

A creatively cut pumpkin basket is a colorful centerpiece for a fall table. Cut out two opposite top quarters of the pumpkin, leaving the stem and a narrow strip as the basket handle. Zigzag the bottom edges, then hollow out the base. Place a block of wet floral foam inside. Position two glass votive holders in the foam, then surround the candles with fall blooms and leaves.

Natural Beauty

Gourds in all shapes and colors easily become seasonal vases. Cut a hole large enough to accommodate a couple of florist tubes. Insert flower stems and other foliage into tubes. Place tubes into gourds.

Thanks a Dot

Thanksgiving guests appreciate cheerful home accents as they gather for the grandest dinner of the year. This artful painting technique is invitingly fun and festive.

Take-Home Treats

Tall terra-cotta flowerpots are ample holders for a handful of party mix, candy, or other goodies. Place food in clear food bags, tie with jute, and set it into each painted flowerpot.

Service with a Smile

Wood serving pieces show off a multitude of coordinating dots. Keep paint away from areas where it will touch food directly and hand-wash all hand-painted pieces.

Details, Details

Carry out the cheery theme to each guest's place. Paint dots onto ribbon to use as napkin ties. Dot plate chargers and precut and painted wood hearts. These accents take little time to accomplish and make the table look dramatic.

Dotalicious

Although turquoise, orange, and shades of gold make a stunning presentation for Thanksgiving, choose whatever colors you like to splash across the table.

Follow the Rules

Bottles from crafts stores come in a variety of shapes, colors, and sizes. Use their outlines to guide the size and placement of painted dots. To make scalloped lines, use a fine paintbrush to carefully outline a series of dried painted dots.

Message Board

Paint a framed insert with chalk paint for a message board to greet every season. Before inserting the chalkboard into the frame, paint the frame and let it dry. Use dowels, pencil erasers, and tips of paintbrush handles dabbed into acrylic paint to dot layers of dots onto the frame, letting dry between layers.

Treasure Box

Small unfinished wooden boxes, available in crafts stores, make sweet gifts for guests to take home. Personalize each one by writing a note telling each guest why you are thankful he or she is in your life. Paint each box to coordinate with the table decor so they'll long remember the special effort you put into making Thanksgiving memorable.

Grand Stand

A shadow box, such as this one that can hang on a wall, displays miniature pumpkins with style.

Perky Pumpkin

Use a playful dot-painting technique to coat a pumpkin in contrasting colors. Most uncut pumpkins last for weeks. For year-after-year use, paint an artificial pumpkin.

In a Twinkling
Putka Pods

Wall Flower

Putka pods are intriguing dimensional centers for felt flowers in autumnal hues. To make flowers, cut two 1×5-inch strips from wool felt. Tie one strip around the center of the other; trim ends even. Weave one "petal" through an opening in a wire basket to secure. Hot-glue a putka pod in the center of each flower. For leaves, fold a piece of green wool felt in half and cut a leaf shape, leaving the fold uncut. Pull the ends through the wire to secure. Tie a jute bow below the bouquet.

Beribboned Place Card

Layered scrapbook papers create place cards in a jiffy. Tie a ribbon bow around the front of each card, then hot-glue a putka pod in the center for the finishing touch.

Seasonal Sensation

Vintage glass jars offer charm and safety as candleholders. Place a pillar candle in the center and carefully pour putka pods around it, being extra careful to keep pods well below the wick. Tie a ribbon around the neck of the jar.

Textural Coat

A tin pail decorated with putka pods glued to the surface, some in flower patterns, is a rustic container for wheat, grasses, or flowers.

trims

BURSTING WITH JOY

REFRESH

Bring on holiday spirit with festive decorations that brighten every room of the house.

Seasonal Sensation

For sophisticated Christmastime style, try black and white and red all over. For sparkle, join silver to the palette.

Mantel Magic
Carry out the color scheme with the hearth and mantel dressed in elegant fanfare.

Santa Surprise

In lieu of stockings, use holiday hat boxes tied with a bow. These sturdy cardboard versions, available in crafts stores, are easy to fill and make a lovely display leading up to the big opening.

To the Point

Dramatize the edge of a mantel with embellished napkins placed on point. To trim one corner, sew on a lightweight glittered snowflake with a large jingle bell in the center. If the napkin tends to slip, stick rings of painter's tape on the underside of the fabric.

Truly Ornamental

This stunning picture makes a grand statement yet is quite easy to achieve. Paint the top three quarters of a 24×36-inch stretched canvas with black acrylic. Paint the remainder of the canvas pearlescent white; let the paint dry. Using this photo as a guide, hot-glue traditional-size plastic silver glitter ornaments (with hangers removed) to the canvas in a triangular tree formation. Add smaller red plastic ornaments atop the silver for a trunk along with a red glittered topper as shown. For accents, glue on tiny glittered white and silver foam balls from a crafts store.

Opening Sensation

Make a grand statement from first entrance by dressing the front door with shimmering trim. Wire together several artificial silver evergreen branches. Add a silver snowflake and finish with a generous red and white bow.

Elegant Invitation

With deep red poinsettias as the main attraction, this tabletop is a flurry of decorative accents to make any holiday get-together outstanding.

CHEERS

Place Card Replacement

Direct guests to their places at the table with initials that gracefully adorn smooth place mats. A length of gem embellishment from an adhesive roll leads to each dimensional letter sticker.

Party Tags

Guests can I.D. stemware when each one has a distinctive tag. Tie stems with cording, threading through tags if possible. Use an adhesive dot to affix each tag to the foot if desired.

Notes of Cheer

Stand small frames by each place setting to deliver a word of holiday cheer. Hot-glue a scrapbook message embellishment to the front, backing with cardstock if needed to cover the frame opening. Add a small ribbon bow as a finishing touch. To add glimmer to the table, sprinkle dimensional crafts-store gems, keeping gems away from table edges.

Grand Tie

A fancy pendant makes a beautiful tie-on as a napkin ring. Make a ring from wide decorative trim and hot-glue the ends together for the ring base. Then use cording to tie the pendant around the ring. Find pendants with jewelry supplies in crafts stores or with buttons in fabric stores.

ho ho ho

O Christmas Tree

A white tree gets compliments galore decked in white lights with ornaments in red, silver, clear glass, and a bit of black. Wrap gifts in coordinating papers and bows for striking continuity.

Clearly Dazzling

Adhesive gems make it easy to craft ornaments in any color combination. To edge a round glass ornament, purchase gems that are affixed to a circular strip of adhesive. Then arrange large gems, snowflake style, in the center.

Glad Tidings Baskets

Transform glittered gift baskets, often used as favor holders, into tree ornaments filled with decorative silvery picks. Just wrap wire stems in a circle to fit the bottom of the basket. Tape in place to secure.

Jingle All the Way

Large snowflake jingle bells reflect Christmas lights and add sparkle to the tree. To dress them up in a jiffy, press an adhesive gem to the center of the design. In place of garland, use strands of beads, hung swag-style, on branches. Buy them in myriad colors at party stores.

Initial Accents

Set the stage for your holiday decorating style with that just-right wreath that welcomes guests. The focal point for each of these wreaths is a family initial.

Totally Traditional

The gilded initial adds glamour to the center of this evergreen wreath. Trim the initial by making a small arrangement with artificial sprigs of holly and berries along with a trio of small ornaments for a splash of color. Hot-glue the trim in place and wire the initial to the wreath with matching wire.

Wonderfully Whimsical

This wreath add-on takes its cue from the initial. For a whimsical look, choose a letter with scrolls or juvenile appeal. Trace the letter onto patterned paper and cut out. Brush the letter with decoupage medium and press the cutout in place; let dry. Hot-glue a vintage plastic figurine to the letter wherever it best fits. Add a sprig of artificial greenery and a small bow alongside the figure.

Simply Contemporary

This flat letter from a crafts store makes a bold statement covered with metallic textured scrapbooking paper. Trace the letter onto the paper and cut out. Brush the letter with decoupage medium and press the cutout in place; let dry. Hot-glue a Christmas trim, such as this reindeer, to the letter, then wire it onto the wreath. Add a satin bow and matching jingle bell as an introduction to the color scheme that awaits beyond the front door.

Tidal Rave
As if the current brought them to shore, seashells add soft panache to a holiday table. Marry them with bright white, silver, and pastels to keep the feel light and airy.

Inspired by the Sea

Organic shapes and textures gathered from the beach make unexpected holiday trims. Layer shells and starfish with pastel glitter for an enchanting coat.

Star Studded

Guests will feel special and welcome with these place cards around the table. Fold cardstock into a tent and add a rectangle of white, edged with silver glitter, for each name. Glitter a starfish and add a gem to the center. Hot-glue the trim to the card as shown.

Favor A Go-Go

Favor guests with lovely reminders of the evening. Trim a pastel paper cup with a silver chenille stem hot-glued below the rim. For the focal point, add a ribbon bow and starfish ornament at the top. Place candies in a plastic candy bag, secure with a snippet of chenille stem, and place into the cup.

Plate Appeal

Group a trio of shells for flower petals, then hot-glue together. Brush the shells with decoupage medium, then sprinkle with pastel glitter. If the shells have ridges, wipe the glitter away from the raised areas with your finger; let dry. Apply glitter to a small shell for the flower center; let dry. Hot-glue the small shell to the center of the flower. Glue the flower to the rim of a plate charger. Trim opposite corners with starfish coated in glitter.

Seeing Double

Two layers of starfish create a brilliant starburst. Coat each shape with glitter, then let dry. Hot-glue the two starfish together as shown. Coat a jingle bell with silver glitter; let dry. Hot-glue the bell to the ornament center and an eye pin to the back of one arm. Thread the pin with narrow ribbon for hanging.

Graceful Garland

Starfish appear ethereal on a snow-white tree. Coat the shapes with decoupage medium and then sprinkle with glitter. Keep the palette simple by using two colors and alternating them on cording for a garland. When decoupage medium is dry, hot-glue an eye pin with a large eye to the back of one arm. Thread with cording, space equally, and knot each starfish in place.

Dollar Delights

Sand dollars have a natural hole for hanging. Coat with decoupage medium and sprinkle with white glitter. When dry, coat just what will be the top half of the sand dollar with decoupage medium, then sprinkle with pastel glitter; let dry.

Going Green

Start holiday decorating with the rich traditional color of evergreen.

Alluring Lights

Green votive cups vie for attention on green glittered snowflakes. While these are preglittered snowflake picture frames, you can get the same look by coating snowflake ornaments with green glitter. To coat, brush snowflake with decoupage medium, then sprinkle with green glitter. When dry, hot-glue plastic gems to the tips.

Jingle Bell Candle

A clear glass vessel shows off the glitter and sparkle of a multitude of jingle bells while providing ample room for a large pillar candle. The assortment of sizes and textures of bells creates visual interest.

Graceful Vase

Paint a coordinating vase using the technique as for the glasses (see Beautifully Banded, opposite). Referring to the photo as a guide, make a dotted "stem" with the handle end of a paintbrush dipped into white glass paint. Add brushstroke flourishes and holly leaves. For larger dots, use a pencil eraser dipped into paint. Let the paint dry.

Beautifully Banded

Give glasses handpainted flair. To keep designs straight, place a rubber band around the glass before painting. Using a small round brush and white glass paint, make equally spaced brushstrokes above and below the rubber band as shown in Photo A. Let the paint dry, then remove the rubber band. Dip the handle end of the paintbrush into the paint and dot between the brushstrokes as shown in Photo B. Let the paint dry. Cure the paint and wash the glasses as recommended by the paint manufacturer.

Simply Stated

Practice writing with a paintbrush on paper. Then use a small brush and white glass paint to paint "joy" or other word on a mug. Dip the handle end of the brush into paint to add dots. Let the paint dry. Cure the paint and wash mugs as recommended by the paint manufacturer.

Woolly Wonderland

Felting with wool is hot during snow season. These distinctly different approaches open your imagination to crafting possibilities.

Woodland Friends

Needle-felting is like sculpting; instead of clay you use wonderfully soft, billowy dyed wool. It takes practice, but the wonderful thing about felting is that you can always revise it. Pull off a bit here or there, or add wool over the top of a spot you'd like to reshape. The more you poke the needle into the fibers, the tighter it becomes and the more detail you can bring out.

FOX

WHAT YOU NEED

Felting pad
36- and 38-gauge felting needles
100% wool batting or roving in red-orange, cream, and black (batting is fluffier/loftier and easier to felt with; but roving, wool in long billowy strips, also works well)

WHAT YOU DO

1. Pull off about a 2½-inch-diameter tuft of red-orange roving.
2. Roll an oval shape for the body. Roll the tuft between your hands for a few seconds to make the shape a bit more compact. Use the 36-gauge felting needle to felt and the 38-gauge to hold piece in place. Repeatedly push the 36-gauge needle down through the fibers. The tiny barbs on the felting needle bind the fibers together tighter and tighter each time you push the needle in and out. Be careful! The needles are sharp, which is why you use two needles—one to hold the wool in place with your fingers out of the way.
3. Make the fox head using a 1-inch-diameter tuft. Form it into a ball and felt with needle to shape.
4. For legs, pull off four separate ½-inch-diameter tufts and roll them. Felt each piece into tighter, small tube shapes. Add a bit of brown/black wool to the ends of the legs. Tip: Pull small amounts of brown/black and wrap around legs, then felt with needle.
5. For the tail, pull off a 1-inch-diameter piece of wool and roll into another tube shape, slightly larger than the legs. Roll and shape tail to points at both ends. Add a bit of cream wool to the end of tail. To blend colors, drag the tip of the needle across the top of the wool fibers, gently pulling a bit of one color into the next (in this case, cream into the orange). You can also grab a wispy amount of cream wool to create a gradual transition of white-tipped tail into orange.
6. To attach the pieces, hold the head onto one end of the body, then use the felting needle through both pieces, working your way around the base or neck of the fox until the pieces are stuck together. Reinforce the joint with a small amount of roving wrapped around and felted in to help make joint areas smooth. Attach legs and tail to the body using the same process.
7. To shape the fox head, add a small bit of orange onto head for the long nose, shape into a cone, then add a tiny dot of black for nose. Add cream to the neck, front, and underside of fox.
8. To finish the fox, add two triangle shapes for ears, two dots of brown/black for eyes, and a thin line for a mouth. To make a mouth, take a scant amount of wool; roll between fingers into a black thread. Attach with a needle at various points.

BUNNY

WHAT YOU NEED

Felting pad
36- and 38-gauge felting needles
100% wool batting or roving in cream, pink, and brown-black

WHAT YOU DO

1. Follow the same process/technique used for the fox, creating body, legs, and ears. The bunny legs are about half the size of the fox; however, bunny ears are taller with a bit of pink inside, instead of cream, and bunny tail is a ¼-inch-diameter ball of cream wool.

RACCOON

WHAT YOU NEED

Felting pad
36- and 38-gauge felting needles
100% wool batting or roving in gray and charcoal/black

WHAT YOU DO

1. Follow the same process/technique used for the fox and bunny, creating body, legs, and ears. For the raccoon tail, use strips of rolled black roving wrapped around to create stripes. Add charcoal/black roving over the face to create a masked appearance.

TREE

WHAT YOU NEED

Felting pad
36- and 38-gauge felting needles
100% wool batting or roving in green and cream
Undyed wool batting pillow fiberfill material
4⅕-inch-diameter tuft of filler white, roll between palms, then felt into a 6-inch-tall cone

WHAT YOU DO

1. Wrap green wool around tree cone, felting it with needle until the white filler stuffing is covered. Add snow using slightly rolled cream wool, circling around the tree. Use needle in an upward motion to attach at different points to create a scalloped, draping effect.
2. String seed beads onto thread in short sections and stitch to tree as shown.

Scenic View

Bright tones and beaded details make this felted scene one to admire.

WHAT YOU NEED

Tracing paper and pencil
Scissors
$8\frac{1}{2}$×11-inch piece of snowflake felt
$8\frac{1}{2}$×11-inch piece of white felt
Wool felt in three shades of green, yellow, blue, orange, pink, red, purple, brown, and gray
Wool roving in blue, purple, and pink
Felting needle and needle felting mat/brush
Sewing needle
Light blue embroidery floss
White thread
Beading needle and silver seed beads
2 black seed beads
$8\frac{1}{2}$×11-inch picture frame

WHAT YOU DO

1. Trace the patterns on page 158 onto tracing paper; cut out. Cut snowbanks from white felt, trees from green, deer from brown, and tree trunks from gray. Cut small white circles from white felt for snowflakes, from yellow for tree toppers, and from a mix of colors for round ornaments and tree stripes.
2. Arrange large snowbank on snowflake background, aligning bottom edges; tack in place with running stitches along top edge as shown. Layer remaining snowbanks; tack in place in same manner.
3. Use the felting needle and mat/brush to felt ornaments and stripes to trees as instructed by the manufacturer. Place trees, one at a time, on white felt and secure in place using the felting technique; trim a narrow border.
4. Place trees on background where shown and felt in place. Add gray tree trunks. Felt yellow circles to white and trim narrow borders. Add to tree tops.
5. Felt deer to background; add three tiny white dots to back.
6. Thread beading needle. Sew gold beads to tree with round ornaments. For garlands, thread needle with a 24-inch length of white thread and knot the ends. Bring the needle up through the back at the edge of a tree. Thread on enough silver seed beads to reach opposite side, draping the beads. Sew a few white felt dots to snowflake background, attaching each with a bead in the center.
7. Use black seed beads to sew on an eye and nose to the deer.
8. Remove the glass from frame. Insert felt piece into frame; replace backing.

Nice and Easy

In minutes, make a collection of ornaments to trim the tree or give as gifts. Use the patterns on page 157 to cut the tree or wreath shape from dark green wool felt. Felt dots of light green wool felt onto wreath. Felt tree and wreath shapes onto light green wool felt. For tree, add a 1-inch-square brown trunk $\frac{1}{4}$ inch from tree bottom. Trim narrow borders to leave light green outlines around wreath and tree. For tree, use needle and thread to sew on purchased beaded felt balls in a zigzag to resemble garland. For wreath, cut a 12×$\frac{1}{4}$-inch strip from red felt and tie into a bow. Stitch it to wreath bottom along with two leaves cut from light green wool felt and a trio of beaded balls. Stitch a yarn loop at the top for hanging.

Perfect Harmony

Natural materials, subtle colors, and creativity blend for an unassuming holiday welcome.

Noteworthy

Hang a small chalkboard from a wreath to let visitors know your whereabouts or to write a greeting to those who enter. Weave burlap ribbon and battery-operated lights through the greenery for a warm homespun touch.

Cozy Up

Place the dining table next to windows to catch winter light. Adorn the table with natural tones and sprigs of greenery for carefree elegance.

Cody

New Heirlooms

Place settings have natural appeal with paper rosette napkin rings and leaf-shape name cards. To make the napkin ring, use the pattern on page 156 to cut the leaf place card from cardstock. To make the flower, cut circles of varying sizes from vintage papers. Pinch the bottom center of the circle to gather, twisting and folding the bottom. For a more full flower, use more than one circle. Add a bit of hot glue to the center bottom tail. Cut a piece of twine to tie around a folded napkin. Hot-glue the flower and leaf place card to the twine at the midpoint. Tie the twine around the napkin, knotting it on the underside.

Recycled Adornments

Paper leaves made from vintage book pages and sheet music decorate the artificial pine and floral tablerunner. Use the pattern on page 156 to cut the leaves.

Word Play

A playful message adds whimsy to a chalkboard in an antique frame. Set amid mercury glass and glittered deer, the seasonal sentiment is an appropriate backdrop at the head of the table.

What Lies Below

Create a table runner in a jiffy by laying opened sheet music beneath a centerpiece arrangement. Use several sheets to run the length of the table.

Hot Spot
Set up a hot cocoa station for all to enjoy. The enlarged recipe behind the shelves provides instruction and graphic interest.

Time Frame

An Advent calendar made from a gray-painted board attached to a vintage window frame marks passing days. Cup hooks hold manila tags numbered with stickers. Each day in December, choose an ornament from a nearby bowl to hang on the corresponding day of the calendar.

Snow Much Fun

With wide grins and twinkling eyes, these snow friends inspire everyone to share in the cheerful spirit of the season.

Front Door Greeter

This jolly gent is a welcome sight even after the holidays. Make the papier-mâché head just as the tabletop figures are made (opposite and pages 62–63), replacing the body with a 1-inch dowel painted red, then wrapped with ribbon.

Making Merry

Thin wooden letter cutouts hang from a garland that can be read from afar. Trace each letter on a different color of glittered paper; cut out. Use decoupage medium to adhere the cutouts to the letters. Drill holes in each upper corner of letters, then use cording to tie the letters onto long lengths of beaded and tinsel garland.

Happy-Go-Lucky

Propped on a mantel or hanging on the wall, this fun-loving scene can be enjoyed all winter. Use the lid of a round cardboard box for the base. Cut a foam ball in half for the snowman. Cut the trees, trunks, and hat from 1-inch-thick plastic foam. Using the photo for placement, hot-glue pieces to the lid. Use small plastic foam balls for the tree toppers. Use instant papier-mâché (just add water) from crafts stores to cover the entire scene. Shape a small pointed nose on the snowman. Let papier-mâché dry. Paint lid with white acrylic paint; let dry. Paint eyes, eyelashes, hat, and mouth black. Paint trees green, the toppers yellow, the trunks brown, and the nose orange. When dry, lightly brush the tops of all colored areas with white paint. Hot-glue trims, such as chenille stems, ribbon, felt snowflakes, and buttons, to the trees and snowman.

Good Friends, Good Times

Let the party begin! Jolly snow folk characters welcome guests to the table with open arms

Fancy That, a Fancy Hat

Full-size felt hats play on a snowman theme. Whether upright or flipped upside down with a snow character nestled inside, these hats are extra-special. To trim one, wrap a band of ribbon around the hat; hot-glue ends in place. Cut a 6×3-inch strip from a vintage book page and pleat every ¼ inch along the long end; fold in half. Dip one edge of "fan" in glue and sprinkle with silver glitter. Hot-glue the fan to the hat at the band seam. Cut a small felt snowflake in half and layer and hot-glue two buttons to the center. Paint the top edges white; let paint dry. Hot-glue the trim to the center of the paper fan.

All Dressed Up and Ready for Snow

Easy-to-do trims give papier-mâché snow guys and gals personality. To make bases, press a foam ball onto any size plastic bottle. Remove the ball and use a table knife to remove the area where indented. Hot-glue the foam ball to the bottle. Use instant papier-mâché to cover snowman shape, adding a short pointed nose; let dry. Paint the figure with white acrylic paint. Add pink cheeks, orange nose, and black eyes and mouth. When dry, brush the top of the nose with white and add a dot to each eye. Using the photos for inspiration, "dress" each snow figure, hot-gluing details in place. Hot-glue stick arms to each side of the snow characters. Gently paint the top of each stick white; let dry.

The Big Day
Honor Christmas day with a festive "25" displayed for all to see. Choose cardboard or wood numbers that are thick enough to stand on their own. Trace around the numbers onto heavy wrapping or scrapbook paper; cut out. Use decoupage medium to adhere the paper to the numbers. Shape silver chenille stems to outline each number, then hot-glue in place.

Temporary Tidings
No need to buy holiday stemware when stickers do the trick. Press letter or seasonal motif stickers to goblet edges, avoiding the rim. For added fun, tie a pair of small plastic ornaments to each stem with cording.

Rim Trim
Give paper plates a face-lift with shimmering garland trim. Hot-glue lengths of garland to the underside of each paper plate, allowing trim to show around the edge.

Hats Off
Felt doll hats are just the right size to hold a handful of wrapped candies. Before filling, paint the underside of the brim edge with white paint to resemble a dusting of snow; let dry. Line hat with tissue paper and fill with treats.

Mr. and Mrs.

These snow characters frolic in evergreen branches. Nestled in paper-wrapped cardboard cones, the snow couple is made from plastic foam balls covered in papier-mâché. To hang, thread narrow wire through each hat and twist the ends together to secure.

Girly Girl

Make a gift box that's sure to be used as a holiday decoration for years to come. Use instant papier-mâché to cover the lid of a round cardboard box. Shape the facial features, such as small papier-mâché balls for the eyes and mouth, a pointed nose, and arched eyebrows. Let the papier-mâché dry thoroughly. Paint the lid with white acrylic paint; let dry. Add pink cheeks, blue shadows, orange nose, and black eyes, eyelashes, and mouth. When dry, brush the top of the nose with white and add a dot to each eye and mouth piece. Hot-glue a length of feather boa to the bottom edge of the lid, adding felt snowflakes and a jingle bell accent. Cover the box bottom with wrapping paper.

Magic Season

Christmas is all about kids, caring, and creating memories—not to mention gorgeous decorating that lasts well before and long after the final ho-ho-ho.

Instant Upgrades

Plain cedar greenery is elegant with only a super affordable dress-up: bay leaves spray-painted gold. It's the same story with any everyday wreath. Embellish it with gold ornaments and a wide satin ribbon bow.

Thin Is In

Try thinning out tree branches before decorating. Ornaments and garland will drape beautifully and show through lavishly. Sprinkle color, such as the green shown here, around the tree for a uniform appearance.

Great Garland

Christmas is for kids! Give your young artists cool materials to work with and their paper chains will draw oohs and aahs. Help them choose scrapbook papers in a limited palette to blend with your decorating scheme.

Personal Attention

A cross-stitched monogram makes an ordinary stocking special. If you don't sew, get the look with easy iron-on letters. Leave the cuff unadorned, placing the monogram in the center of the stocking for a fun twist.

Package Palette

Continue your holiday color scheme into gift wrap. Papers can have holiday motifs or not—either works. Top packages with generous ribbon and fancy fiber bows to make each gift as beautiful as the one beside it. Keep tags simple for an elegant display beneath the tree branches.

Birds of a Feather Felted Together

Inspired by the great wintry outdoors, these decorations are to be enjoyed the entire snowy season.

Bright Visitors

Berried branches and a crafts store nest make natural perches for brilliant red cardinals. For snowy effects, fill a clear glass vase with Epsom salt to hold branches upright and line the nest with a tuft of batting.

All Is Calm

Using nature's palette as a guide, these marking pen and painted plates mimic the centerpiece branches. Use greenery to cradle plates with seasonal aroma.

A

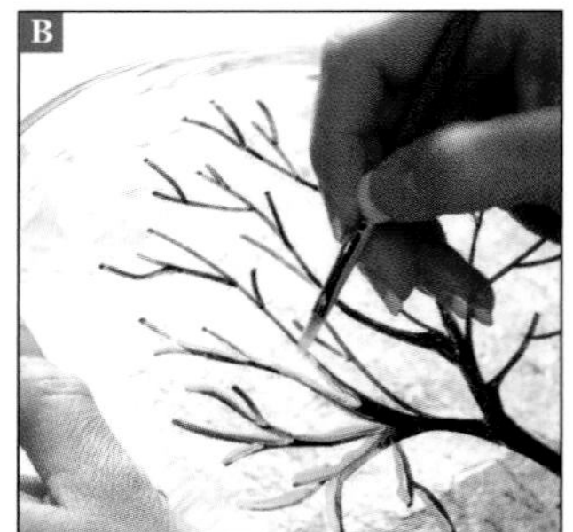
B

C

D

For the Birds

Who would guess that these clear glass plates get the start of their wonderful design with a marking pen? On the back side of a plate, use a permanent black marking pen to draw a simple branched tree, using Photo A as a guide. Use white glass paint to edge the top of each branch as shown in Photo B. Randomly paint red bird shapes on branches as shown in Photo C, then draw in black beaks. Dip the handle tip of the paintbrush into white paint and dot around tree, as shown in Photo D. Let the paint dry. Cure and wash the painted plates according to the paint manufacturer's instructions.

Felted Feathered Friends

Adorn bare branches with bright red felted birds. To make one, trace the patterns on page 155 and cut out. Use the patterns to cut the shapes from red wool felt. Lay the head piece on the body as shown in Photo A and felt together using a felting needle and mat. Roll the rounded end into a head shape and gently felt together as shown in Photo B. Fold the body in half and felt together, avoiding the tail feathers, as shown in Photo C. Attach a wing to each side as shown in Photo D. Use a needle and black thread to make French knot eyes as shown in Photos E and F. Cut a tiny triangle from yellow felt and hot-glue it to the head for a beak.

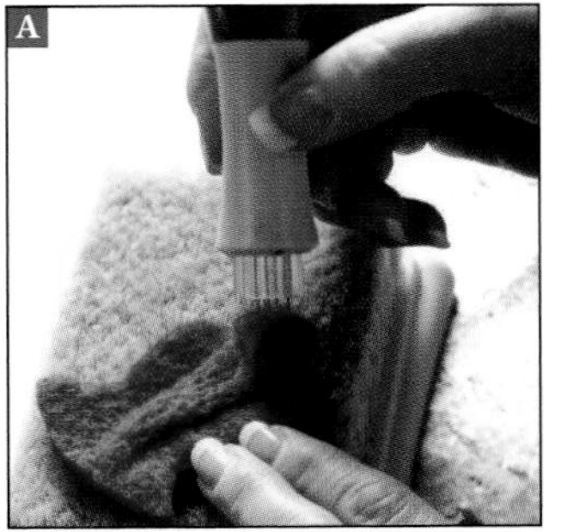

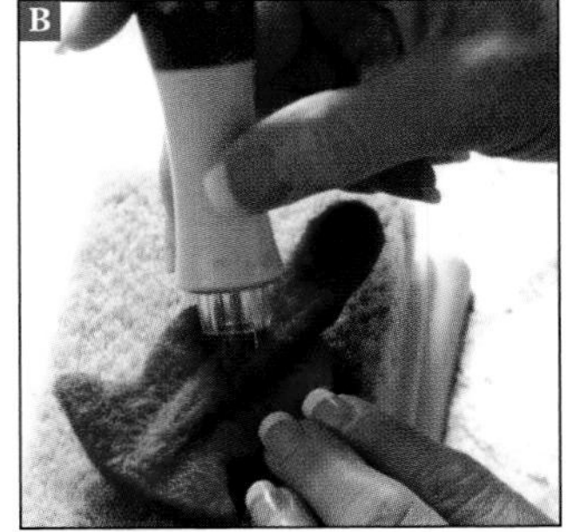

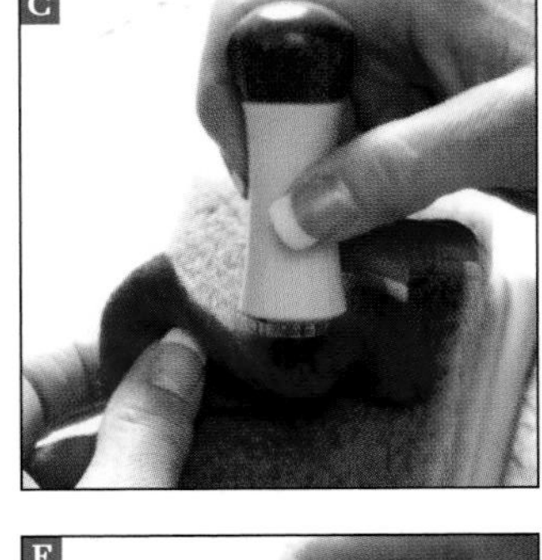

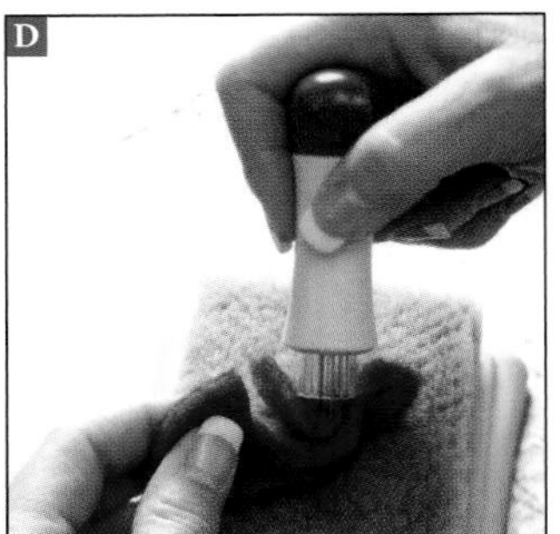

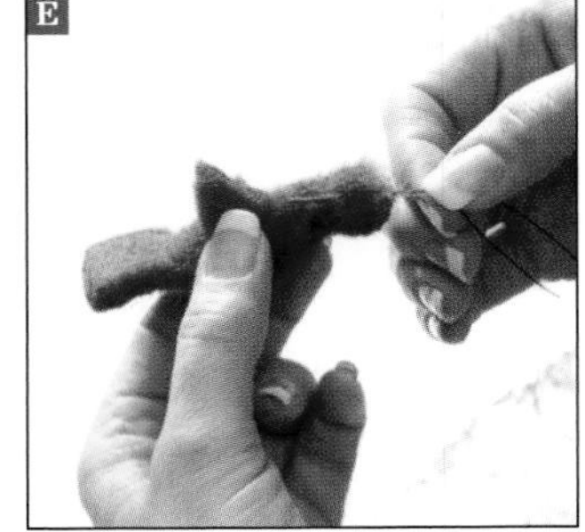

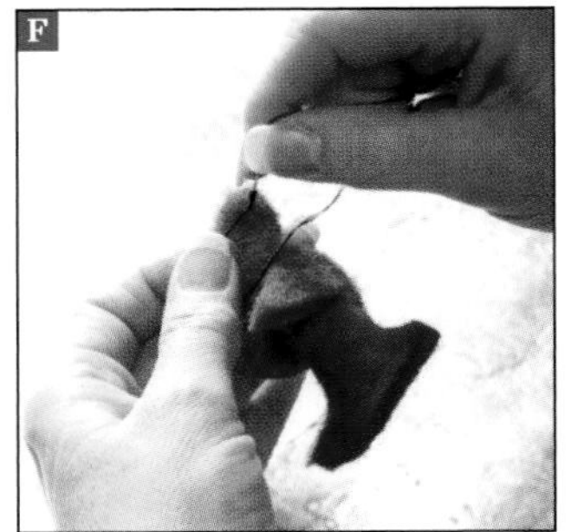

Merry Miniatures

This tabletop display recalls an era of simple times, simple joys. Recreate a scene using minimal resources of time and materials.

Make a Scene

Dollhouse miniatures set in jars create fascinating scenes. Make them Christmassy by gluing on miniature lights, bottlebrush trees, and beads. Hot-glue the pieces inside the jar, then surround with white glitter. Trim the lids with ribbon, cord, and scrapbook embellishments.

Country Quaint

Vintage-looking jars from a crafts store give these snow globes old-fashioned charm. Hot-glue the miniature characters and bottlebrush trees, old or new, to jar bottoms, then spoon in glitter all around for snow. Replace lids and tie with jute as the finishing element.

Frosty Frolic

Light blue and creamy white set the stage for frosty decorations to admire well after New Year's.

Deck the Wall

For something new, create a long-lasting wreath with fabric instead of greenery. Trace a maple leaf or other favorite leaf to cut shapes from pastel linen fabrics. Glue the fabric leaves to a wire form, then tie a long velvet ribbon bow to the top for flourish.

Warm Wishes

Perfect for hostess gifts, these little beauties add extra sparkle to the holidays. To make one, wrap a silver votive holder with velvet ribbon; hot-glue in place. Affix a mini painted pinecone to the center.

Hunt and Gather

Tabletop trees are a big space saver and a no-mess alternative to a traditional Christmas tree. Secure tree branches in a container with florist's foam, then cover the top with moss. For decorations, hot-glue spray-painted pinecones, velvet acorns, and silver stars to the branches. Weave chiffon ribbon through the branches.

Ornamental Treasures

Silk velvet acorn ornaments have a luxurious look and are simple to make. Gather a small piece of fabric around a cotton ball, then tie it with thread at the top to hold. Hot-glue a natural acorn cap to the top. Attach a hanging ribbon to use them as tree ornaments or add a name tag to use at place settings.

Seasonal Flourish

Wrapped packages reflect a classic style. Juxtapose textures, such as velvet, ribbons, and shiny silver paper, with natural elements.

Natural Instincts

For a new take on naturals, spray-paint pinecones in hues of blue and silver. Display the pinecones in a neutral color bowl to let the pinecones stand out.

Burlap Leaves

Cut long leaf shapes from light blue and white burlap or sheer woven fabric, then stitch stem ends to ribbon. Drape from a mantel to soften the edge.

Modern Woodland

Rustic meets refined at this table. Brush white paint on the tips of pinecones, glue to velvet ribbon, and secure clusters to chair backs with stick-on plastic hooks.

New Year Cheer

Bring on the new year with a holiday party that's as easy as 1-2-3. One great drink, pretty flowers, and a belle-of-the-ball decoration.

Ring It In

Dress up a plain tissue bell with a glittery clapper. Cut off the bottom ringer piece to make room for an ornament. Open the bell and secure with tabs. Coat with gold glitter spray; let dry. Close bell. Tie a long ribbon to hanger on ornament, then snuggle ball into bottom of bell. Secure ribbon in center of bell fold with dots of glue; also glue along the cardboard edge before hanging.

Bye-Bye Buds

As guests head home for the evening, let each take part of the party home. Snip off a bloom from the centerpiece to offer it in a wineglass filled ever so slightly with water. Make a happy New Year cuff for the base of the goblet by cutting rings of paper to fit around the stem. Glue the layers together, slit one side to slip onto the stem, and write a simple message. Embellish the add-on with a satin rose bud and ribbon bow hot-glued to one side.

Rock On

Get a candy and cocktail in one, using flutes accompanied by rock candy swizzle sticks.

Cool Cocktail

A signature drink makes the party special—and easy. In a large pitcher (to serve eight), mix 2 cups ruby red grapefruit juice and 1 cup chilled tangerine- or clementine-flavored vodka; slowly stir in a 750-ml bottle of chilled pink Prosecco. Rub the rims of cocktail glasses with an orange wedge, then dip lightly in coarse red and gold sugar.

In a Twinkling Frosted Fast

Just-for-You Jar

A simple initial, created using a sticker, personalizes a treat jar. Press the sticker onto jar. Coat the jar with etching cream and etch according to the manufacturer's instructions. Rinse off the cream, remove the sticker, and dry the jar. Outline the letter using glitter glue; let dry. Tie the neck with a sheer ribbon bow.

Fire and Ice

Icicles form along the edge of a votive holder. Use a brush to paint icicle shapes along the top. Etch glass following the manufacturer's instructions; rinse. Use clear and silver glitter glue to enhance the etched designs, keeping glue away from the rim. Let the glue dry.

Merry Ornaments

Etch subtle messages of cheer into glass ornaments. Use letter stickers to spell words on ornaments. Carefully brush on etching cream, feathering edges to make a band around entire ornament. Once etched, rinse off the cream and remove the sticker.

Polka-Dot Plate

Fun any time of the year, these etched plates add sparkly interest to plain clear glass plates. Place round stickers on one side, then align the same size stickers on the other. Etch both sides of the plate. Rinse the plate and remove the stickers to reveal the polka dots.

Snowflake Sensation

Make wintertime glasses fun with snowflakes etched into the surface. Use masking tape to section off area to be etched. Place round stickers and binder reinforcements in any snowflake formation. Brush etching cream onto the area between tape lines and let set according to the manufacturer's instructions. Rinse off the cream and remove stickers and tape to unveil the designs.

PEPPERMINT BLONDIES
recipe on page 115

food

THE HOLIDAY TABLE

INDULGE

Treat family and friends to once-a-year foods that truly make the season special. Savory nibbles, sweets and treats, and a holiday feast bring everyone together.

POMEGRANATE PAVLOVA WITH PISTACHIOS AND HONEY
recipe on page 104

PICK-A-TOPPER APPETIZER FLATBREADS recipe on page 94

Nibbles and Sips

The best party food invites mixing and mingling as you nosh. These finger foods and festive drinks fit that definition perfectly.

SAGE AND BACON MEATBALLS
recipe on page 94

Pick-a-Topper Appetizer Flatbreads

WHAT YOU NEED

1¼ cups warm water (105°F to 115°F)
2 tablespoons olive oil
1 package active dry yeast
1 teaspoon sugar
3¼ to 3½ cups all-purpose flour
1 teaspoon salt
Cornmeal
Toppers (see recipes that follow; each recipe makes enough to top 1 flatbread)

WHAT YOU DO

1. In a medium bowl combine warm water, olive oil, yeast, and sugar. Stir to dissolve yeast. Let stand about 10 minutes or until foamy.
2. Meanwhile, in a large bowl combine 2¾ cups of the flour and the salt. Stir yeast mixture into flour mixture. Using a wooden spoon, stir in as much of the remaining flour as you can.
3. Turn out dough onto a lightly floured surface. Knead in enough remaining flour to make a soft dough that is smooth and elastic (3 to 5 minutes).
4. Place dough in an oiled bowl, turning once to coat surface of dough. Cover and let rise in a warm place until double in size (45 to 60 minutes).
5. Preheat oven to 450°F. Punch down dough. Turn out dough onto a lightly floured surface. Divide dough into nine equal portions. Cover and let rest for 10 minutes. Roll each portion into a 9×4-inch oval. (Cover remaining dough while working so it stays moist.)
6. Sprinkle a baking sheet with cornmeal. Place three ovals crosswise on the baking sheet. Top each with a topper. Bake about 10 minutes or until golden. Repeat with remaining dough. Makes 9 flatbreads.

Apple-Bacon Topper: Top a flatbread with 5 or 6 thin slices apple. Sprinkle with 1 slice crumbled, crisp-cooked bacon. Drizzle with 2 teaspoons maple syrup. If desired, sprinkle with 2 tablespoons shredded white cheddar cheese.
Blue Cheese-Pear Topper: In a medium skillet, heat 1 tablespoon vegetable oil over medium-low heat. Add ½ cup thinly sliced sweet onion; cook until tender and golden. Spread onion on flatbread. Top with 5 or 6 thin pear slices and sprinkle with 2 tablespoons crumbled blue cheese.
Rosemary-Potato Topper: Sprinkle flatbread with 2 tablespoons shredded Gruyère or Raclette cheese. Top with 5 or 6 slices cooked red-skin potato. Sprinkle with ½ teaspoon snipped fresh rosemary, dash sea salt, and a few grinds black pepper. Drizzle with 1 to 2 teaspoons olive oil.
Sausage-Green Olive Topper: Spread 2 tablespoons pizza sauce on flatbread. Top with 2 tablespoons cooked Italian sausage and 1 tablespoon sliced green olives. Sprinkle with 2 tablespoons shredded mozzarella cheese.
Chutney-Grape-Pistachio Topper: Spread 2 tablespoons bottled chutney on flatbread. Top with 10 seedless red grapes, halved, and 1 tablespoon coarsely chopped pistachios.
Sweet Potato-Sage Topper: Brush flatbread with 2 teaspoons olive oil. Top with 5 or 6 thin slices sweet potato, 2 teaspoons snipped fresh sage, and 2 teaspoons maple syrup. Sprinkle 1 tablespoon crumbled, crisp-cooked pancetta over. If desired, sprinkle with sea salt and ground black pepper.
Thai Peanut-Chicken Topper: In a small bowl combine ¼ cup shredded cooked chicken, 2 tablespoons bottled peanut sauce, and 1 tablespoon shredded carrot. Spoon over a dough oval. Sprinkle with 1 green onion, bias-sliced.
Barbecue Chicken Topper: Spread 2 tablespoons bottled barbecue sauce on a dough oval. Top with ¼ cup shredded cooked chicken and 1 tablespoon chopped green sweet pepper. Sprinkle with 2 tablespoons shredded Monterey Jack cheese.
Balsamic-Cremini-Goat Cheese Topper: In a medium skillet heat 2 teaspoons vegetable oil over medium heat. Cook ½ cup sliced cremini mushrooms until nearly tender. Add 1 tablespoon balsamic vinegar; continue cooking until liquid evaporates and mushrooms are tender. Spread on flatbread. Sprinkle with 2 tablespoons crumbled goat cheese and ½ teaspoon fresh thyme leaves. Just before serving, drizzle with 1 teaspoon balsamic vinegar.

Sage and Bacon Meatballs

WHAT YOU NEED

24 slices bacon
2 eggs, lightly beaten
2 cups whipping cream
1½ cups finely chopped red onion
½ cup ground toasted pecans or almonds
6 tablespoons snipped fresh sage
¼ teaspoon salt
¼ teaspoon ground black pepper
2 pounds ground pork
2 cloves garlic, minced
Fresh sage leaves (optional)

WHAT YOU DO

1. Preheat oven to 350°F. In a large skillet cook 8 slices of the bacon over medium heat until crisp; drain on paper towels. Cook remaining bacon for 4 to 5 minutes or just until beginning to brown, turning once. Drain on paper towels. Reserve 2 tablespoons drippings in skillet. Finely chop the crisp bacon; set aside.
2. In a large bowl combine eggs, ¼ cup of the whipping cream, 1 cup of the red onion, nuts, ¼ cup of the sage, salt, and pepper. Add pork and three-fourths of the finely chopped bacon; mix well.
3. Shape into 32 meatballs. Place meatballs in a single layer in a roasting pan. Bake, uncovered, about 25 minutes or until done (160°F). Cool 15 minutes.
4. Thread 2 meatballs and 1 slice of the partially cooked bacon onto a 4-inch skewer, weaving bacon around meatballs. Repeat with remaining meatballs and bacon slices. Place on the unheated rack of a broiler pan. Broil 3 to 4 inches from the heat for 4 to 5 minutes or until bacon is crisp, turning once.
5. Meanwhile, for sauce, in the reserved drippings cook the remaining ½ cup onion and the garlic over medium heat for 2 to 3 minutes or until tender. Stir in the remaining whipping cream and the remaining snipped sage. Bring to boiling; reduce heat. Simmer for 5 minutes or until thickened. Stir in the remaining finely chopped bacon.
6. Arrange meatball kabobs on a platter. If desired, garnish with sage leaves. Serve with sauce. Makes 16 servings.

CHAMPAGNE-CITRUS PUNCH

Champagne-Citrus Punch

WHAT YOU NEED

1 6-ounce can frozen orange juice concentrate, thawed (⅔ cup)
½ 6-ounce can frozen lemonade concentrate, thawed (⅓ cup)
½ 750-milliliter bottle (about 1⅔ cups) sweet white wine or blush wine (such as Riesling or white Zinfandel), chilled
1 cup cold water
1 750-milliliter bottle champagne, chilled
Fruited Ice (optional)

WHAT YOU DO

In a large punch bowl combine orange juice concentrate and lemonade concentrate. Add wine and the cold water, stirring to combine. Carefully add champagne, but do not stir. If desired, float Fruited Ice in punch.

Fruited Ice: Cut several pieces of fruit (such as limes, Key limes, kumquats, oranges, blood oranges, lemons, and/or blackberries) into halves, quarters, or slices. Arrange in an 8-inch square baking pan. Pour enough ginger ale (about 2½ cups) over the fruit in the pan to cover. Cover and freeze for 6 hours or until firm. Remove from freezer and let stand 20 to 30 minutes. Break into chunks. Add to punch bowl.

Hot Scarlet Wine Punch

For a special occasion, garnish each cup of punch with cranberries threaded like beads onto cocktail skewers.

WHAT YOU NEED

2 inches stick cinnamon
4 whole cloves
1 32-ounce bottle cranberry juice (4 cups)
⅓ cup packed brown sugar
1 750-milliliter bottle white Zinfandel or dry white wine
Whole fresh cranberries (optional)

WHAT YOU DO

1. For spice bag, cut a double thickness of 100-percent-cotton cheesecloth into a 6-inch square. Place cinnamon and cloves in the center of the cloth. Bring the corners together and tie closed with clean kitchen string. In a 3½- or 4-quart slow cooker combine spice bag, cranberry juice, and brown sugar.
2. Cover and heat on low-heat setting for 3 to 4 hours or on high-heat setting for 1 to 1½ hours.
3. Remove and discard the spice bag. If using low-heat setting, turn slow cooker to high-heat setting. Stir wine into punch. Cover and heat for 30 minutes more. Serve immediately or keep warm, covered, on low-heat setting up to 2 hours. Ladle punch into heatproof cups. If desired, garnish with cranberries on skewers. Makes 14 (4-ounce) servings.

Creamy Bacon-Filled Crescents

WHAT YOU NEED

4 slices bacon, finely chopped
1 8-ounce package cream cheese, softened
½ cup freshly grated Parmesan cheese
2 to 4 green onions, thinly sliced (¼ cup)
1 tablespoon milk
2 8-ounce packages refrigerated crescent rolls (8 rolls each)
1 egg
1 tablespoon water
1 to 2 teaspoons poppy seeds
Fresh chives (optional)

WHAT YOU DO

1. Preheat oven to 375°F. In a skillet cook bacon until crisp; drain. Line an extra-large baking sheet with parchment paper; set aside. For filling, in a medium bowl stir together bacon, cream cheese, Parmesan cheese, green onions, and milk until nearly smooth; set aside.
2. Unroll and separate crescent rolls into 16 triangles. Spread each triangle with some of the filling. Roll up from a wide end of the triangle. Place on prepared baking sheet.
3. In a small bowl beat egg with water until combined. Brush crescents with the egg mixture; sprinkle with poppy seeds.
4. Bake about 12 minutes or until puffed and light golden brown. If desired, garnish with chives. Serve warm. Makes 16 servings.
Make-Ahead Tip: Prepare as directed through Step 2. Cover and chill on prepared baking sheet up to 5 hours. (Or freeze in a single layer until firm. Place in a self-sealing plastic freezer bag and freeze for up to 1 month.) To bake frozen crescents, preheat oven to 375°F. Line a baking sheet with parchment paper. Arrange frozen filled crescents in a single layer on prepared baking sheet. Brush and bake as directed for 14 to 16 minutes or until golden and heated through. If you'd like to freeze the baked crescents for later, cool on wire racks. Freeze in a single layer until firm. Place in a self-sealing plastic freezer bag and freeze up to 3 months. To reheat crescents, preheat oven to 350°F. Line a baking sheet with parchment paper. Arrange frozen baked crescents in a single layer on prepared baking sheet. Bake for 8 minutes.

Marinated Olives

WHAT YOU NEED

2 cups black and/or green olives, pitted, rinsed, and drained
½ cup extra virgin olive oil
2 3×½-inch strips of lemon peel
½ cup lemon juice
4 to 6 cloves garlic, sliced
2 teaspoons snipped fresh oregano or 1 teaspoon dried oregano, crushed
1 bay leaf
½ teaspoon crushed red pepper

WHAT YOU DO

1. In a 1-quart jar with a screw-top lid combine olives, olive oil, lemon peel, lemon juice, garlic, oregano, bay leaf, and red pepper. Cover and shake to coat olives with marinade. Refrigerate for 2 days, gently rotating jar occasionally.
2. Before serving, let stand at room temperature for 1 to 2 hours. Remove olives from marinade. Store in the refrigerator for up to 2 weeks.
Makes 2 cups.

Caramelized Onion-Blue Cheese Dip

WHAT YOU NEED

1 tablespoon olive oil
1 large sweet onion, halved and cut into thin slivers
8 ounces cremini mushrooms, chopped
½ 8-ounce package reduced-fat cream cheese (Neufchâtel), softened
⅓ cup crumbled blue cheese
¼ cup fat-free milk
1 teaspoon snipped fresh thyme or sage
⅛ teaspoon salt
⅛ teaspoon freshly ground black pepper
Pear slices, melba toast, and/or whole grain crackers

WHAT YOU DO

1. In a large nonstick skillet heat olive oil over medium heat. Add onion. Cover and cook in hot oil for 10 minutes, stirring occasionally. Uncover and add mushrooms. Cook, uncovered, for 8 to 10 minutes or until mushrooms are tender and onion is golden brown, stirring occasionally.
2. Add cream cheese, blue cheese, milk, thyme, salt, and pepper to onion mixture. Cook and stir over low heat until cheese is melted. Serve warm with pear slices, melba toast, and/or whole grain crackers. Makes 8 (¼-cup) servings.

HOT SCARLET
WINE PUNCH

N-
ENTS

CARAMELIZED
ONION-BLUE CHEESE DIP

MARINATED OLIVES

ROSEMARY ROASTED LOIN OF PORK
recipe on page 100

Festive Feast

Gather friends and family for a multicourse memory-making meal—much of which can be made ahead.

CREAMY BRIE-TOPPED POTATOES
recipe on page 100

Rosemary Roasted Loin of Pork

WHAT YOU NEED

- 1 cup sliced leeks (3 medium)
- 2 tablespoons snipped fresh basil
- 3 to 4 teaspoons snipped fresh rosemary
- 2 cloves garlic, minced
- ½ teaspoon salt
- ¼ teaspoon freshly ground black pepper
- 2 tablespoons olive oil
- 1 2½-pound boneless pork top loin roast (single loin)
- 2 sprigs fresh rosemary

WHAT YOU DO

1. Preheat oven to 375°F. In a food processor combine leeks, basil, snipped rosemary, garlic, salt, and pepper. Add 1 tablespoon of the oil. Process until mixture forms a chunky paste.
2. Cut loin in half lengthwise. Spread half of the leek mixture on the cut sides of the loin. Place cut sides together and tie tightly with 100-percent-cotton kitchen string. Thread rosemary sprigs through the string on the roast. Using a skewer, poke holes into the top and sides of the roast; brush the remaining 1 tablespoon oil over the roast. Spread the remaining leek mixture over the roast. Place roast on a rack in a shallow roasting pan.
3. Roast for 1 to 1½ hours or until an instant-read thermometer inserted into thickest part of the roast registers 155°F. Transfer the roast to a platter. Cover with foil. Let stand for 15 minutes before carving. Temperature of meat after standing should be 160°F. Makes 8 servings.
Make-Ahead Tip: Prepare roast as directed through Step 2. Cover and chill up to 24 hours. Let stand at room temperature for 30 minutes. Continue as directed in Step 3.

Creamy Brie-Topped Potatoes

Full of potatoes, cheese, and smoky bacon, this decadent dish originated in the French Alps. Although the classic dish often features rich and creamy Reblochon cheese, Brie has a similar texture and nutty taste.

WHAT YOU NEED

- 3 pounds Yukon gold potatoes (about 9 medium)
- ½ teaspoon salt
- ¼ teaspoon ground black pepper
- 5 slices thick-sliced bacon, chopped
- 1 large onion, thinly sliced
- 2 cloves garlic, minced
- ⅓ cup dry white wine
- 2 teaspoons snipped fresh thyme
- ¼ cup chicken broth
- ¼ cup whipping cream
- 2 8-ounce rounds Brie cheese
- Fresh thyme sprigs (optional)

WHAT YOU DO

1. Preheat oven to 350°F. Grease a 2-quart gratin dish or rectangular baking dish; set aside. In a covered Dutch oven cook potatoes in enough simmering salted water to cover for 25 minutes; drain. Rinse with cold water; drain again. Slice potatoes about ¼ inch thick. Sprinkle with salt and pepper. Layer half the potatoes in the prepared dish.
2. Meanwhile, in a large skillet cook bacon over medium heat for 1 minute. Add onion and garlic; cook and stir about 5 minutes or until bacon is crisp and onion is tender. Drain off fat. Carefully add wine to bacon mixture. Simmer, uncovered, until wine is almost evaporated. Stir in the snipped thyme.
3. Spoon bacon mixture over potatoes in dish. Layer with remaining potatoes. Pour broth and cream over layers. Cut cheese crosswise into ¼-inch-thick rectangles; layer on potatoes.
4. Bake about 40 minutes or until potatoes are tender and cheese is lightly browned. If desired, garnish with fresh thyme sprigs. Makes 12 servings.

Orange Browned Butter Carrots and Cauliflower

WHAT YOU NEED

- 2 pounds small carrots with tops or peeled fresh baby carrots
- 1 medium head cauliflower, trimmed and cut into 1-inch florets (6 cups florets)
- Salt
- Ground black pepper
- ½ cup butter
- 1½ teaspoons snipped fresh thyme
- ½ teaspoon finely shredded orange peel
- ½ cup dry-roasted pistachio nuts, chopped

WHAT YOU NEED

1. Trim carrots, leaving about 1 inch of the tops. Halve or quarter any large carrots. Place a large steamer basket* in a large Dutch oven or an extra-large skillet filled with 1 inch of water. Add carrots. Bring water to boiling; reduce heat. Simmer, covered, for 5 minutes. Add cauliflower; continue to steam for 5 to 7 minutes or just until carrots and cauliflower are tender. Using a slotted spoon, place vegetables on a serving platter; sprinkle with salt and pepper. If necessary, cover with foil to keep warm.
2. Meanwhile, in a small saucepan melt butter over low heat. Add thyme. Continue heating for 15 to 20 minutes or until butter turns a deep golden color. Stir in orange peel. Drizzle over carrots and cauliflower. Sprinkle with pistachios. Makes 12 servings.
***Test Kitchen Tip:** If you don't have a large enough steamer basket, Dutch oven, or skillet, cook the carrots and cauliflower half at a time. Cover to keep warm while cooking the remaining vegetables.
Make-Ahead Tip: Cut and trim carrots and cauliflower as directed in Step 1; cover and chill up to 24 hours. Prepare browned butter as directed in Step 2; pour into a microwave-safe storage container; seal. Chill up to 24 hours. To serve, steam vegetables as directed. Meanwhile, microwave butter mixture on 100 percent power (high) for 1 to 2 minutes or until melted and hot, stirring occasionally. Drizzle over carrots and cauliflower. Sprinkle with pistachios.

ORANGE BROWNED BUTTER CARROTS AND CAULIFLOWER

BUTTERNUT SQUASH AND CARROT SOUP

Butternut Squash and Carrot Soup

This creamy vegetable soup tastes indulgent but is actually quite healthful. Top it with toasted pumpkin seeds for an added treat.

WHAT YOU NEED

3 cups peeled, diced butternut squash (about 1 small squash)
2 cups thinly sliced carrots (4 medium)
¾ cup thinly sliced leek or chopped onion
1 tablespoon butter or margarine
2 14.5-ounce cans reduced-sodium chicken broth
¼ teaspoon ground white pepper
¼ teaspoon ground nutmeg
¼ cup half-and-half or light cream
Crème fraîche or dairy sour cream (optional)
Toasted pumpkin seeds (pepitas) (optional)
Fresh tarragon sprigs (optional)

WHAT YOU DO

1. In a large covered saucepan cook squash, carrots, and leek in hot butter over medium heat about 8 minutes, stirring occasionally. Add broth. Bring to boiling; reduce heat. Simmer, covered, for 25 to 35 minutes or until vegetables are very tender. Cool slightly.
2. Place one-third of the squash mixture in a food processor or blender. Cover and process or blend until almost smooth. Repeat with remaining squash mixture. Return all of the mixture to saucepan. Add white pepper and nutmeg; bring just to boiling. Add half-and-half; heat through. If desired, garnish each serving with crème fraîche, pumpkin seeds, and/or fresh tarragon. Makes 6 servings.

Apple, Celery Root, and Fennel Salad

A sprinkling of shredded blue cheese adds contrasting flavor this salad. To make it easy to shred the cheese, buy it whole (rather than crumbled) and freeze it for 30 minutes before shredding.

WHAT YOU NEED

¼ cup walnut oil or sunflower oil
2 tablespoons cider vinegar
1 tablespoon lemon juice
1 small shallot, finely chopped (2 tablespoons)
1 teaspoon honey mustard
¼ teaspoon salt
¼ teaspoon ground black pepper
4 cups torn curly endive
1 head butterhead (Boston) lettuce, torn
1 red apple, cored and cut into matchstick-size pieces (1¾ cups)
1 small celery root, peeled and cut into matchstick-size pieces (2 cups)
1 small fennel bulb, trimmed, halved, and thinly sliced (1 cup)
2 ounces shredded blue cheese or feta cheese
⅓ cup chopped walnuts, toasted

WHAT YOU NEED

1. For the dressing, in a screw-top jar combine oil, cider vinegar, lemon juice, shallot, honey mustard, salt, and pepper. Cover and shake well.
2. In a large bowl combine endive and butterhead lettuce. Add three-fourths of the dressing; toss to coat. Divide greens among salad plates.
3. In the same bowl combine apple, celery root, and fennel. Toss with remaining dressing to coat. Divide evenly over greens. Top each salad with blue cheese and walnuts. Makes 6 servings.
Make-Ahead Tip: Prepare and store dressing in the refrigerator up to 3 days. Bring dressing to room temperature before using. Continue as directed in Step 2.

APPLE, CELERY ROOT, AND FENNEL SALAD

PESTO PARKER HOUSE ROLLS

Pesto Parker House Rolls

WHAT YOU NEED

1 cup lightly packed fresh basil
2½ to 2¾ cups all-purpose flour
1 package active dry yeast
1¼ cups milk
2 tablespoons sugar
2 tablespoons olive oil
1 teaspoon salt
1 egg
1 cup whole wheat flour or white whole wheat flour
½ cup finely shredded Parmesan cheese (2 ounces)
⅓ cup pine nuts, toasted and chopped
4 cloves garlic, minced

WHAT YOU DO

1. Place basil in a food processor. Cover and pulse with several on/off turns until finely chopped; set aside. In a large mixing bowl combine 1 cup of the all-purpose flour and the yeast. In a medium saucepan heat and stir milk, sugar, oil, and salt until warm (120°F to 130°F). Add milk mixture to flour mixture along with the egg. Beat with an electric mixer on low to medium speed for 30 seconds, scraping bowl constantly. Beat on high speed for 3 minutes. Using a wooden spoon, stir in whole wheat flour, basil, and as much of the remaining all-purpose flour as you can.
2. Turn dough out onto a lightly floured surface. Knead in enough of the remaining all-purpose flour to make a soft dough that is smooth and elastic (3 to 5 minutes total). Shape dough into a ball. Place in a lightly greased bowl, turning once to grease surface of dough. Cover and let rise in a warm place until double in size (about 1 hour).
3. Punch down dough. Turn out onto a lightly floured surface. Cover; let rest for 10 minutes. Grease two large baking sheets; set aside. In a small bowl combine cheese, pine nuts, and garlic. Roll dough to ¼-inch thickness. Use a floured 3-inch round cutter to cut into rounds. Reroll scraps as necessary.
4. To shape rolls, make a crease in each dough round slightly off center. Spoon about 1 teaspoon of the cheese mixture onto the small half of the dough round. Fold larger half of dough round over the smaller half. Place rolls, larger halves on top, 2 inches apart on prepared baking sheets. Cover and let rise until nearly double in size (about 30 minutes).
5. Preheat oven to 375°F. Bake about 10 minutes or until golden. Transfer rolls to wire racks. Cool slightly; serve warm. Makes 28 rolls.

Pomegranate Pavlova with Pistachios and Honey

WHAT YOU NEED

6 egg whites
Dash salt
Dash cream of tartar
1½ cups sugar
1½ teaspoons vanilla
1 teaspoon lemon juice
2½ teaspoons cornstarch
1½ cups pomegranate juice
¼ cup honey
1 tablespoon lemon juice
1½ cups whipping cream
1 tablespoon sugar
1 cup pomegranate seeds
¼ cup pistachio nuts, coarsely chopped

WHAT YOU NEED

1. Allow egg whites to stand at room temperature for 30 minutes. Meanwhile, line a baking sheet with parchment paper. Draw a 9-inch circle on the paper. Invert paper so the circle is on the reverse side.
2. Place rack in center of oven. Preheat oven to 250°F. For meringue, in a large mixing bowl beat egg whites, salt, and cream of tartar with an electric mixer on medium speed until soft peaks form (tips curl). Add 1½ cups sugar, 1 tablespoon at a time, beating on high until stiff peaks form (tips stand straight). Beat in ½ teaspoon of the vanilla and 1 teaspoon lemon juice. Sift cornstarch over egg white mixture; fold in gently.
3. Spread meringue over circle on paper, building up edges slightly to form a shell. Bake for 1 hour (do not open oven door while baking). Turn off oven; let meringue stand in oven with door closed for 1 hour.
4. For pomegranate syrup, in a small saucepan combine pomegranate juice, honey, and 1 tablespoon lemon juice. Bring to boiling over medium; reduce heat. Boil gently, uncovered, for 30 to 40 minutes or until syrup is reduced to ½ cup. Transfer to a bowl; cool.
5. In a large chilled mixing bowl beat whipping cream, 1 tablespoon sugar, and remaining 1 teaspoon vanilla with chilled beaters of mixer on medium speed until stiff peaks form (tips stand straight).
6. Carefully lift meringue off paper and transfer to a serving plate. Spread with the whipped cream. Sprinkle with pomegranate seeds; drizzle with the pomegranate syrup. Sprinkle with pistachio nuts. Serve immediately. Makes 12 servings.

POMEGRANATE PAVLOVA
WITH PISTACHIOS AND HONEY

Holiday Brunch

Rouse sleepyheads from their beds with a simple celebratory Christmas brunch that's easy on the cook.

GINGERBREAD CINNAMON BUNS
recipe on page 108

POMEGRANATE SPRITZERS
and PEACH BELLINIS
recipes on page 108

Gingerbread Cinnamon Buns

WHAT YOU NEED

- ¼ cup warm water (105°F to 115°F)
- 2 packages active dry yeast
- ½ cup evaporated milk
- ⅓ cup molasses
- ¼ cup packed brown sugar
- 1 egg, lightly beaten
- 2 tablespoons vegetable oil
- ½ teaspoon salt
- 3¾ to 4 cups all-purpose flour
- ¼ cup packed brown sugar
- 2 tablespoons granulated sugar
- 1 teaspoon ground cinnamon
- ½ teaspoon ground ginger
- ¼ teaspoon ground cloves
- 2 tablespoons butter, softened
- 1 recipe Spiced Glaze
- Sugared cranberries* (optional)

WHAT YOU DO

1. In a large bowl combine warm water and yeast, stirring to dissolve yeast. Let stand for 5 minutes. Stir in evaporated milk, molasses, ¼ cup brown sugar, egg, oil, and salt. Stir in as much of the flour as you can.

2. Turn dough out onto a lightly floured surface. Knead in enough of the remaining flour to make a moderately soft dough that is smooth and elastic (3 to 5 minutes total). Shape dough into a ball. Place in a lightly greased bowl, turning once to grease surface. Cover and let rise in a warm place until double in size (1 to 1½ hours).

3. Punch down dough. Turn out onto a lightly floured surface. Cover and let stand for 10 minutes. Lightly grease a 13×9×2-inch baking pan; set aside. For filling, in a small bowl combine ¼ cup brown sugar, the granulated sugar, cinnamon, ginger, and cloves.

4. Roll dough into a 12×8-inch rectangle. Spread dough with butter. Sprinkle with filling, leaving 1 inch unfilled along one long side. Roll up rectangle, starting from the filled long side. Pinch dough to seal seams. Cut into 12 slices. Arrange rolls in the prepared pan. Cover and let rise in a warm place until nearly double in size (about 45 minutes).

5. Preheat oven to 350°F. Bake for 22 to 25 minutes or until golden brown. Cool in pan on a wire rack for 5 minutes. Drizzle with Spiced Glaze. If desired, sprinkle with sugared cranberries. Serve warm. Makes 12 buns.

Spiced Glaze: In a small bowl stir together 1½ cups powdered sugar, 1 tablespoon milk, ½ teaspoon ground cinnamon, and ½ teaspoon vanilla. Stir in additional milk, 1 teaspoon at a time, to make glaze a drizzling consistency.

***Test Kitchen Tip:** To make sugared cranberries, roll frozen cranberries in granulated sugar.

Pomegranate Spritzers

WHAT YOU NEED

- 1 cup pomegranate juice, chilled
- 1 750-milliliter bottle champagne or sparkling wine of choice, chilled
- Pomegranate seeds (optional)*

WHAT YOU DO

1. Add 2 tablespoons pomegranate juice to each of 8 champagne flutes. Pour Champagne into each glass to serve. If desired, garnish each glass with pomegranate seeds. Makes 8 servings.

Nonalcoholic Pomegranate Sparkler: Prepare as directed, except substitute sparkling apple juice for the Champagne.

***Test Kitchen Tip:** For pomegranate seeds, score an X in the top of a pomegranate. Break apart into quarters. Working in a bowl of cool water, immerse each quarter. Use your fingers to loosen the seeds from the white membrane. Discard peel and membrane. Drain seeds. Cover and chill up to 24 hours.

Peach Bellinis

WHAT YOU NEED

- 3 cups peach nectar
- 1½ cups Prosecco, champagne, or sparkling water
- Ice cubes
- 6 small strawberries

WHAT YOU DO

In a large pitcher stir together peach nectar and Prosecco. Place ice in 6 champagne glasses; pour peach nectar mixture over ice. Place a strawberry in each glass.

Make-Ahead Tip: Chill peach nectar and Prosecco separately up to 2 hours. Prepare strawberries. Cover and chill up to 2 hours. To serve, assemble as directed. Makes 6 servings.

Crab and Swiss Strata

WHAT YOU NEED

- 6 English muffins, split
- 3 tablespoons butter, softened
- 2 6½-ounce cans crabmeat, drained, flaked, and cartilage removed, or 12 ounces frozen cooked crabmeat, thawed
- ¾ cup shredded Swiss cheese (3 ounces)
- ¾ cup shredded cheddar cheese (3 ounces)
- 2 tablespoons capers, drained
- ½ cup finely chopped onion
- 1 tablespoon butter
- ¼ cup dry sherry
- ½ teaspoon Worcestershire sauce
- 6 eggs, beaten
- 1 cup milk
- 1 tablespoon Dijon-style mustard
- 1 tablespoon snipped fresh parsley
- Salt and ground black pepper

WHAT YOU DO

1. Spread English muffin halves with the 3 tablespoons butter. Line a greased 2-quart rectangular baking dish with half the muffins, buttered side up. In a medium bowl combine crabmeat and cheeses. Layer crab mixture over muffins in dish; sprinkle with capers. Top with remaining muffins, buttered sides up.

2. In a large skillet cook onion in 1 tablespoon butter over medium heat for 5 minutes or until tender. Stir in sherry and Worcestershire. Bring just to boiling; remove from heat.

3. In a medium bowl combine eggs, milk, mustard, parsley, dash salt, and dash pepper. Stir in onion mixture. Carefully pour over the layers in the baking dish. Press muffins lightly with back of a large spoon to moisten muffins on top. Cover; chill overnight.

4. Preheat oven to 350°F. Bake, uncovered, for 50 minutes or until muffins are browned and a knife inserted near the center comes out clean. Let stand 10 minutes before serving. Makes 8 servings.

CRAB AND SWISS STRATA

HONEY-RUM FRUIT SALAD

Eggnog Muffins

WHAT YOU NEED

2¼ cups all-purpose flour
1 cup sugar
2 teaspoons baking powder
½ teaspoon ground nutmeg
2 eggs, lightly beaten
1 cup dairy eggnog
½ cup butter, melted and cooled
1 teaspoon vanilla
½ teaspoon rum extract
1 recipe Nutmeg-Streusel Topping

WHAT YOU DO

1. Preheat oven to 375°F. Grease twelve 2½-inch muffin cups or line with paper bake cups; set aside. In a medium bowl combine flour, sugar, baking powder, and nutmeg. Make a well in the center of the flour mixture; set aside.
2. In another bowl combine eggs, eggnog, butter, vanilla, and rum extract. Add egg mixture all at once to flour mixture. Stir just until moistened (batter should be lumpy). Spoon batter into prepared muffin cups, filling each two-thirds full. Sprinkle Nutmeg-Streusel Topping over muffin batter in cups.
3. Bake for 18 to 20 minutes or until golden and a wooden toothpick inserted in centers comes out clean. Cool in muffin cups on a wire rack for 5 minutes. Remove from muffin cups; serve warm. Makes 12 muffins.
Nutmeg-Streusel Topping: In a bowl combine ⅓ cup flour, ⅓ cup sugar, and ½ teaspoon ground nutmeg. Using a pastry blender, cut in 2 tablespoons cold butter until the topping resembles coarse crumbs.
Make-Ahead Tip: Prepare as directed; cool completely. Place muffins in a single layer in a resealable plastic freezer bag. Seal, label, and freeze up to 2 months. To serve, thaw at room temperature.

Honey-Rum Fruit Salad

A dressing of mint, lime, rum, and honey bathes fresh fruits with refreshing flavor.

WHAT YOU NEED

¼ cup snipped fresh mint
¼ cup lime juice
¼ cup rum or orange juice
¼ cup honey
1 large cantaloupe or honeydew melon
16 ounces fresh strawberries, hulled and halved or quartered
1½ cups green and/or red seedless grapes
4 kiwifruits and/or golden kiwifruits, peeled and cut into ½-inch pieces

WHAT YOU DO

1. For dressing, in a large bowl whisk together mint, lime juice, rum, and honey; set aside.
2. Cut cantaloupe in half and remove the seeds. Use a melon baller to scoop out pulp. In a large bowl combine melon balls, strawberries, grapes, and kiwifruits. Add dressing; toss lightly to coat. Let stand for 15 minutes to blend flavors. Makes 8 servings.
Make-Ahead Tip: Prepare as directed. Cover and chill up to 6 hours.

EGGNOG MUFFINS

MOLASSES COOKIE CUTOUTS
recipe on page 115

PEPPERMINT BLONDIES
recipe on page 115

Sweets and Treats

Make goodies to share (and some for yourself). Choose from an array of seasonal cookies, brownies, and bars—plus a classic candy with a modern twist.

CHOCOLATE HAZELNUT TREES

Molasses Cutouts

WHAT YOU NEED

- ½ cup shortening
- ⅔ cup granulated sugar
- 2 teaspoons freshly grated nutmeg or 1½ teaspoons ground nutmeg
- 1 teaspoon baking powder
- ¼ teaspoon salt
- ½ cup mild-flavor molasses
- 1 egg
- 1 tablespoon cider vinegar
- 2½ cups all-purpose flour
- 1 recipe Royal Icing
- Sanding sugar, nonpareils, and/ or small peppermint candies (optional)

WHAT YOU DO

1. In a large mixing bowl beat shortening with an electric mixer on medium to high speed for 30 seconds. Add granulated sugar, nutmeg, baking powder, and salt. Beat until combined, scraping sides of bowl occasionally. Beat in molasses, egg, and vinegar until combined. Beat in as much of the flour as you can with the mixer. Stir in any remaining flour. Divide dough in half. Cover and chill about 3 hours or until dough is easy to handle.
2. Preheat oven to 375°F. Grease a cookie sheet; set aside. On a lightly floured surface roll half the dough at a time to ⅛ inch thick. Cut dough with 2½- to 3-inch people-shape cookie cutters. Place 1 inch apart on prepared cookie sheet.
3. Bake for 5 to 6 minutes or until bottoms are light brown. Cool on cookie sheet for 1 minute. Transfer cookies to a wire rack; cool completely.
4. Add enough water to Royal Icing, 1 teaspoon at a time, just until icing is thin enough to flow over cookies. Tint frosting as desired. Pipe thinned Royal Icing along edges of cookie to outline dresses, pants, and vests. Pipe more icing onto cookie within outline. Using a small metal spatula or a knife, spread frosting to outlines. If desired, while icing is wet, sprinkle with sanding sugar or nonpareils or decorate with peppermint candies. Makes 36 to 48 cookies.
Royal Icing: In a large mixing bowl stir together one 16-ounce package powdered sugar (4 cups), 3 tablespoons meringue powder, and ½ teaspoon cream of tartar. Add ½ cup warm water and 1 teaspoon vanilla. Beat with an electric mixer on low speed until combined. Beat on high speed for 7 minutes or until stiff. Cover bowl with damp paper towels and plastic wrap. Chill up to 48 hours if needed.
To Store: Place cookies in a single layer in an airtight container; cover. Store at room temperature for up to 2 days.

Peppermint Blondies

WHAT YOU NEED

- 12 ounces white chocolate, chopped
- ½ cup butter
- ½ cup granulated sugar
- 3 eggs, lightly beaten
- 2 teaspoons vanilla
- 1 teaspoon peppermint extract
- 1½ cups all-purpose flour
- 1 cup miniature semisweet chocolate pieces
- 1 recipe White Chocolate-Peppermint Frosting
- Coarsely crushed striped round peppermint candies (optional)

WHAT YOU DO

1. Preheat oven to 350°F. Grease a 13×9×2-inch baking pan; set aside. In a medium saucepan heat and stir white chocolate over low heat until melted and smooth. Remove from heat; stir in butter until melted. Whisk in the granulated sugar, eggs, vanilla, and peppermint extract until smooth. Stir in flour until combined. Spread batter in prepared pan.
2. Bake for 28 to 30 minutes or until top is light brown and sides begin to pull away from pan. Immediately sprinkle semisweet chocolate pieces evenly over bars. Cool in pan on a wire rack.
3. Evenly spread White Chocolate-Peppermint Frosting on cooled bars. If desired, sprinkle with crushed peppermint candies. Makes 32 bars.
White Chocolate-Peppermint Frosting: In a small saucepan heat and stir 6 ounces chopped white baking chocolate over low heat until smooth. Set aside until lukewarm. In a large mixing bowl combine ½ cup softened butter and 1¾ cups powdered sugar. Beat with an electric mixer on low speed until combined. Beat in ⅓ cup sour cream, ½ teaspoon vanilla, ½ teaspoon peppermint extract, and ¼ teaspoon salt. Beat in 1¾ cups additional powdered sugar. Beat in melted white chocolate until combined
To Store: Place bars in a single layer in an airtight container; cover. Refrigerate up to 3 days or freeze up to 2 months.

Chocolate Hazelnut Trees

WHAT YOU NEED

- 2½ cups all-purpose flour
- ¼ cup unsweetened cocoa powder
- ½ teaspoon baking soda
- ¼ teaspoon salt
- ½ cup butter, softened
- ½ cup chocolate-hazelnut spread
- 1 cup sugar
- 2 eggs
- 1½ teaspoons vanilla
- 1 recipe Powdered Sugar Icing (optional)
- Decorating sugars (optional)

WHAT YOU DO

1. In a medium bowl stir together flour, cocoa powder, baking soda, and salt; set aside. In a large mixing bowl beat butter and chocolate-hazelnut spread with an electric mixer on medium to high speed for 30 seconds. Add sugar. Beat until combined, scraping sides of bowl occasionally. Beat in eggs and vanilla. Beat in as much of the flour mixture as you can with the mixer. Using a wooden spoon, stir in any remaining flour mixture. Cover and chill dough about 2 hours or until easy to handle.
2. Shape chilled dough into six logs (10 inches long and ¾ inch in diameter). Wrap logs in plastic wrap and freeze about 30 minutes or until very firm.
3. Preheat oven to 375°F. Using a sharp knife, cut chilled logs into ⅛-inch slices (return logs to freezer if they soften). For each tree cookie, on an ungreased cookie sheet place one slice for a trunk. Centered over that, overlap four slices in a row (overlap by ¼ inch). Add a row of three slices, overlapping each and the row of four. Add a row of two slices in the same manner; add one slice on top. Repeat with remaining dough, spacing trees 2 inches apart on cookie sheet.
4. Bake for 6 to 8 minutes or until edges are firm. Transfer cookies to a wire rack to cool. If desired, drizzle with Powdered Sugar Icing and sprinkle with decorating sugars. Makes 36 cookies.
Powdered Sugar Icing: In a small bowl combine 1 cup powdered sugar and enough milk (4 to 5 tablespoons) to make a drizzling consistency.
To Store: Layer cookies between sheets of waxed paper in an airtight container; cover. Store at room temperature up to 3 days or freeze up to 3 months.

SANTA-SIZE GINGERBREAD COOKIES

Santa-Size Gingerbread Cookies

WHAT YOU NEED

2½ cups all-purpose flour
2½ teaspoons ground ginger
2 teaspoons baking soda
¾ teaspoon ground cinnamon
½ teaspoon salt
⅛ teaspoon freshly grated nutmeg
Dash ground cloves
¾ cup butter, softened
1 cup packed brown sugar
½ cup mild-flavor molasses
1 egg
1 recipe Powdered Sugar Icing

WHAT YOU DO

1. In a medium bowl stir together flour, ginger, baking soda, cinnamon, salt, nutmeg, and cloves; set aside.
2. In a large mixing bowl beat butter with an electric mixer on medium to high speed for 30 seconds. Add brown sugar and molasses. Beat until combined, scraping sides of bowl. Beat in egg. Gradually beat in flour mixture. Cover; chill dough 1 hour or until easy to handle.
3. Preheat oven to 325°F. Line two cookie sheets with parchment paper. Roll ⅓-cup portions of dough into balls. Place 4 or 5 balls 4 inches apart on each cookie sheet. Flatten balls slightly.
4. Bake for 15 to 18 minutes or until edges of cookies are set. Do not overbake. Cool on cookie sheets for 10 minutes. Transfer cookies to a wire rack to cool completely. Spread cookies with Powdered Sugar Icing. Let stand until icing is set. Makes 9 cookies.
Powdered Sugar Icing: In a bowl stir together 1 cup powdered sugar, ¼ teaspoon vanilla, and 1 tablespoon milk. Stir in additional milk, 1 teaspoon at a time, until icing reaches spreading consistency.

Dulce de Leche Fluff Brownies

WHAT YOU NEED

1 cup butter
6 ounces unsweetened chocolate, coarsely chopped
2 cups sugar
4 eggs
2 teaspoons vanilla
1⅓ cups all-purpose flour
½ teaspoon baking soda
1 cup miniature semisweet chocolate pieces
1 13.4-ounce can dulce de leche
1 7-ounce jar marshmallow creme
½ cup chopped pecans, toasted

DULCE DE LECHE FLUFF BROWNIES

WHAT YOU DO

1. In a medium saucepan heat and stir butter and unsweetened chocolate over low heat until mixture is melted and smooth. Set aside to cool.
2. Preheat oven to 350°F. Line a 13×9×2-inch baking pan with foil, extending foil over edges of pan. Grease foil; set aside.
3. Stir the sugar into cooled chocolate mixture. Add the eggs, one at a time, beating with a wooden spoon after each addition just until combined. Stir in the vanilla. In a small bowl stir together the flour and baking soda. Add flour mixture to chocolate mixture; stir just until combined. Stir in semisweet chocolate pieces. Spread batter evenly in the prepared baking pan.
4. Bake for 20 to 25 minutes or until edges are set and center is almost set. Meanwhile, transfer dulce de leche to a small microwave-safe bowl. Microwave on 100 percent power (high) about 1 minute or until softened, stirring once. Transfer baking pan from oven to a wire rack. Immediately spoon mounds of marshmallow creme on hot brownies. Drop spoonfuls of dulce de leche between mounds of marshmallow creme. Let stand a few minutes to soften. Use a knife or thin metal spatula to swirl marshmallow creme and dulce de leche together. Sprinkle with chopped pecans. Cool in pan on a wire rack.
5. Using the edges of the foil, lift uncut brownies out of pan. Cut into bars, wiping knife as needed between cuts. Brownies are best served the day they are prepared. Place any leftover brownies in a single layer in an airtight container; cover. Store in the refrigerator up to 3 days. Makes 32 brownies.

HOLIDAY SEVEN-LAYER BARS

LEMON-PISTACHIO NOUGAT

Holiday Seven-Layer Bars

Use kitchen scissors to snip caramels into small pieces. If the caramels stick to the scissors, lightly coat the scissors with nonstick cooking spray.

WHAT YOU NEED

- ½ cup butter
- 2 cups finely crushed vanilla wafers (48 wafers) or shortbread cookies (33 cookies)
- 1 14-ounce can sweetened condensed milk
- 1 cup butterscotch-flavor pieces, candy-coated milk caramels (such as Sugar Babies), snipped vanilla caramels, semisweet chocolate pieces, or red and green candy-coated milk chocolate pieces
- 1 6-ounce package white baking chocolate, white confectionery bars, chopped, or 1 cup white baking pieces
- 1 cup mixed dried fruit bits, coarsely chopped dried apricots, golden raisins, dried cranberries, or dried cherries
- 1⅓ cups flaked or shredded coconut
- 1 cup unsalted mixed nuts or lightly salted roasted cashew pieces, coarsely chopped

WHAT YOU DO

1. Preheat oven to 350°F. Line a 13×9×2-inch baking pan with foil, extending the foil over the edges of the pan. Place butter in prepared pan; place in oven about 5 minutes or until butter is melted. Tilt pan to coat bottom evenly. Sprinkle with crushed wafers for crust.
2. Drizzle crust with sweetened condensed milk. Sprinkle with butterscotch-flavor pieces, white chocolate, fruit bits, coconut, and nuts. Press down firmly with back of a spoon.
3. Bake for 25 minutes or until edges are lightly browned. Cool in pan on a wire rack. Use foil to lift from pan. Cut into bars. Makes 30 bars.

Make-Ahead Tip: Prepare as directed. Place bars in a single layer in an airtight container; cover. Refrigerate up to 3 days or freeze up to 3 months.

Lemon-Pistachio Nougat

WHAT YOU NEED

- Butter
- Cornstarch
- 1½ cups sugar
- 1 cup light-color corn syrup
- ½ cup water
- 2 egg whites
- 1 teaspoon vanilla
- 1½ teaspoons finely shredded lemon peel
- ¾ cup chopped pistachio nuts
- Nonstick cooking spray
- Powdered sugar

MILK CHOCOLATE AND CHERRY COOKIES

WHAT YOU DO

1. Line a 9×5×3-inch loaf pan with foil, extending foil over the edges of the pan. Butter foil; sprinkle with a small amount of cornstarch. Set pan aside.
2. In a heavy 2-quart saucepan add sugar, corn syrup, and water. Stir once just to moisten the sugar. Clip a candy thermometer to side of pan. Place over medium heat and bring to boiling without stirring. Continue boiling at a moderate, steady rate until thermometer registers 295°F, hard-crack stage (35 to 40 minutes). Adjust heat as necessary to maintain a steady boil.
3. Remove saucepan from heat. Remove thermometer. In a large bowl* beat egg whites with an electric mixer on medium speed until stiff peaks form (tips stand straight). Gradually pour hot syrup in a thin stream over egg whites, beating with the electric mixer on medium to high speed. (Add mixture slowly without stopping to ensure proper blending; do not scrape down the sides.)
4. Add vanilla. Continue beating on high speed until candy becomes very thick and less glossy (5 to 6 minutes). When beaters are lifted, nougat should fall in a ribbon, mound on itself, then slowly disappear into the remaining nougat.
5. Immediately stir in lemon peel and pistachio nuts. Coat a rubber spatula with nonstick spray. Use the spatula to quickly spoon nougat into the prepared pan. When nougat is firm, use foil to lift it out of pan. Place on a cutting board. Coat a knife with cooking spray. Cut into 24 squares. Lightly coat pieces in powdered sugar. Wrap each piece in plastic wrap. Store in an airtight container at room temperature up to 2 weeks. Makes 24 servings.
***Test Kitchen Tip:** Use a bowl with a rubberized bottom or place a damp kitchen towel or paper towel under mixing bowl to keep it in place so your hands are free to beat the egg white mixture and drizzle in the candy mixture at the same time.

Milk Chocolate and Cherry Cookies

WHAT YOU NEED

2 cups frozen pitted dark sweet cherries (about 42)
½ cup butter, softened
1 cup sugar
¼ teaspoon baking powder
¼ teaspoon baking soda
¼ teaspoon salt
1 egg
1½ teaspoons vanilla
½ cup unsweetened cocoa powder
1½ cups all-purpose flour
1 cup milk chocolate pieces
½ cup sweetened condensed milk
4 teaspoons cherry liqueur or milk

WHAT YOU DO

1. Thaw cherries; pat dry with paper towels. Set aside. Preheat oven to 350°F. In a medium mixing bowl beat butter with an electric mixer on medium to high speed for 30 seconds. Add sugar, baking powder, baking soda, and salt. Beat until combined, scraping sides of bowl occasionally. Beat in egg and vanilla until combined. Beat in cocoa powder and as much of the flour as you can with the mixer. Using a wooden spoon, stir in any remaining flour.
2. Shape dough into 1-inch balls. Place balls about 2 inches apart on an ungreased cookie sheet. Press your thumb into the center of each ball. Place a cherry in each indentation.
3. For frosting, in a small saucepan stir chocolate pieces and sweetened condensed milk over low heat until chocolate is melted. Stir in cherry liqueur. Spoon about 1 teaspoon of the frosting over each cherry.
4. Bake about 10 minutes or until edges are firm. Cool on cookie sheet for 1 minute. Transfer cookies to a wire rack; cool. Makes 42 cookies.
To Store: Layer cookies between sheets of waxed paper in an airtight container. Store in the refrigerator up to 3 days or freeze up to 3 months.

In a Twinkling

In the mix

Confetti Peanut Butter Munchies

In an extra-large bowl combine 7 cups crispy corn and rice cereal and 2 cups pretzel sticks or nuggets. In a small saucepan combine 1 cup semisweet chocolate pieces, ½ cup peanut butter, and ¼ cup butter. Stir over medium-low heat until melted. Remove from heat; stir in 1 teaspoon vanilla. Pour chocolate mixture over cereal mixture. Toss to coat. Place 2 cups powdered sugar in a large resealable bag. Add cereal mixture a portion at a time. Seal bag and shake to coat. Spread mixture on waxed paper; let stand 1 hour or until set. In an extra-large bowl combine cereal mixture, ½ cup chopped dried mango, ½ cup chopped dried pineapple, ¼ cup dried cranberries, and ¼ cup golden raisins. Makes 11 cups.

White Chocolate Snack Mix

In an extra-large bowl combine 2 cups bite-size wheat or rice square cereal or bite-size shredded wheat biscuits, 2 cups broken graham crackers, 2 cups pretzel sticks, 2 cups broken rice cakes, 1 cup tiny marshmallows, 1 cup raisins or dried fruit bits, and 1 cup whole or slivered almonds or cashews. In a medium saucepan combine 1 pound chopped white baking chocolate, ⅓ cup whipping cream, and 1 tablespoon light-color corn syrup. Cook until smooth. Stir in ½ teaspoon almond extract. Pour warm chocolate mixture over cereal mixture. Toss to coat. Immediately spread onto an extra-large piece of waxed paper. Cool until chocolate is set (up to 12 hours). Break into pieces. Makes about 14 cups.

Onion and Garlic Macadamia Nuts

In a large skillet heat 3 tablespoons olive oil over medium heat for 1 to 2 minutes or until very hot. Carefully add 1 tablespoon dried parsley flakes, 1 tablespoon onion salt, 1½ teaspoons sugar, 1½ teaspoons lemon juice, and ¾ teaspoon garlic powder, stirring until combined. Add 3 cups macadamia nuts. Cook and stir for 5 minutes. Drain nuts on paper towels. Cool. Makes 3 cups.

Chili Mixed Nuts

In a small bowl combine 2 tablespoons melted butter, 1 tablespoon chili powder, 1 tablespoon lime juice, and 1 teaspoon garlic salt. In a 15×10×1-inch baking pan combine butter mixture and 3 cups mixed nuts. Toss to coat. Bake in a 325°F oven for 15 minutes, stirring once. Spread on a large piece of foil to cool. Store in an airtight container up to 2 weeks or freeze up to 3 months. Makes 3 cups.

Crunchy Cracker Snack Mix

In a large roasting pan combine 4 cups bite-size cheese crackers and 5 cups snack sticks. Bake in a 300°F oven for 5 minutes. Stir in 3 cups pretzel twists and 2 cups mixed nuts. Pour ½ cup melted butter over all. Sprinkle with one 7-ounce envelope cheese-garlic, Parmesan, or Italian dry salad dressing mix; stir to coat. Bake for 20 minutes, stirring once. Spread on foil to cool. Store in an airtight container up to 1 week. Makes 14 cups.

gifts

MAKE SOMEONE SMILE

WRAP IT UP

Share your time and talents by making gifts to cherish for those you love.

Photo Finish

Old and new family snapshots add a meaningful flourishes to holiday decor. Make these projects as unforgettable gifts for your clan.

All in the Family

Fashion a family tree garland to drape across a mantel or shelf by clipping photos to a length of ribbon. For an orderly trip down memory lane, start with great-great-grandparents at one end of the garland, progressing to the youngest generation.

Tag Team

Photo tags make family gift exchanges extra fun. They pass on a bit of family history and recall special or funny moments. Print digital photos onto cardstock, then crop to any tag shape. Punch a hole and thread with cotton twine or ribbon.

Can-Do Centerpiece

Meet a centerpiece that's easy, inexpensive, and original. Cans wrapped in computer-printed images deliver all three. Skimp a bit on the flowers—the sweet faces are the stars. To make one, print a photo onto cardstock, then crop to fit the can, allowing a small overlap. Hot-glue the edges to the can. If the printout is from an inkjet printer, seal with clear acrylic spray. To prevent the can from rusting, place a glass container inside to hold water for a bouquet.

Well-Plated

Earn rave reviews from family members with photos decoupaged to the underside of salad plates. For a subdued scheme, print color photos in black-and-white or sepia (adding a narrow border if desired) onto vellum. Cut out images and seal with clear acrylic spray. Use a foam brush to apply decoupage medium onto the bottom center of a clear glass plate. Carefully center the right side of the cutout onto the glue. Smooth out air bubbles and let dry. Add two more coats of decoupage medium, allowing to dry between coats. Hand-wash and dry the plates.

Beribboned

Decorate a gift of bread and soup mix with holiday flair. To wrap bread, use decorative-edge scissors to cut a sleeve of parchment paper slightly wider than layered ribbons; wrap bread and tape ends together. Layer natural-tone ribbons and wrap around parchment layer; hot-glue ends together. Tie a narrow ribbon bow through the hole in a wooden tag and hot-glue to the top of the bread. Slip loaf into a cellophane bag to keep it fresh. For soup, hot-glue a ribbon bow and a few snippets of greenery to the lid of a glass container.

CREAMY VEGETABLE-LENTIL SOUP MIX and QUICK SEED BREAD

Gifts of Good Taste

With the abundance of sweets in circulation this time of year, a prettily wrapped gift of soup and bread is a welcome change of pace.

Creamy Vegetable Lentil Soup Mix

WHAT YOU NEED

1 cup dried carrots, corn, peas, sweet peppers, and tomatoes
2 tablespoons dried minced onion
1 tablespoon instant chicken bouillon granules
1½ teaspoons dried thyme, crushed
½ teaspoon ground black pepper
¼ teaspoon garlic powder
¾ cup dried yellow lentils

WHAT YOU DO

Place the dried vegetable mix in a 1-pint jar. In a small bowl stir together the minced onion, bouillon granules, thyme, black pepper, and garlic powder. Spoon over vegetables in jar. Place lentils in a small plastic bag. Place bag on top layer; fasten lid. Attach directions to make Creamy Vegetable Lentil Soup.

To make Creamy Vegetable Lentil Soup: Remove lentils from jar and rinse. Pour remaining contents of jar into a large saucepan. Add the rinsed lentils and 4 cups water. Bring to boiling; reduce heat. Cover and simmer for 20 minutes or until lentils are tender, stirring occasionally. Stir in ¾ cup half-and-half or light cream. Cook and stir over low heat for 1 minute more. Makes 4 servings (5 cups prepared soup).

Quick Seed Bread

WHAT YOU NEED

1½ cups all-purpose flour
½ cup whole wheat flour
¾ cup packed brown sugar
½ cup dry-roasted sunflower kernels
⅓ cup flaxseed meal
2 tablespoons sesame seeds
2 tablespoons poppy seeds
1 teaspoon baking powder
½ teaspoon baking soda
½ teaspoon salt
1 egg
1¼ cups buttermilk or sour milk*
¼ cup vegetable oil
4 teaspoons sesame seeds, poppy seeds and/or dry-roasted sunflower kernels

WHAT YOU DO

1. Preheat oven to 350°F. Grease the bottom and ½ inch up sides of a 9×5×3-inch loaf pan; set aside.
2. In a large bowl stir together flours, brown sugar, ½ cup sunflower kernels, flaxseed meal, the 2 tablespoons sesame seeds, the 2 tablespoons poppy seeds, baking powder, baking soda, and salt. Make a well in center of flour mixture; set aside. In a medium bowl beat egg with a fork; stir in buttermilk and oil. Add egg mixture to flour mixture. Stir just until moistened. Spread in prepared pan. Sprinkle with the 4 teaspoons seeds.
3. Bake for 45 to 55 minutes or until a wooden toothpick inserted near center comes out clean. Cool in pan on a wire rack for 10 minutes. Remove from pan. Cool completely on wire rack. Wrap and store overnight before slicing. Makes 14 servings.

***Test Kitchen Tip:** To make 1¼ cups sour milk, place 4 teaspoons lemon juice or vinegar in a glass measuring cup. Add milk to equal 1¼ cups total liquid; stir. Let stand for 5 minutes before using.

Pasta-Herb Soup Mix

WHAT YOU NEED

2 tablespoons reduced-sodium instant chicken bouillon granules or 6 reduced-sodium chicken bouillon cubes
½ teaspoon dried thyme, crushed
½ teaspoon dried oregano, crushed
½ teaspoon dried rosemary, crushed
½ teaspoon ground black pepper
¼ teaspoon garlic powder
2 cups dried multigrain farfalle pasta
⅓ cup dried chopped onion
½ cup snipped dried tomatoes (not oil-packed)
¼ cup dried chopped green sweet pepper
¾ cup dried porcini mushrooms

WHAT YOU DO

1. In a small bowl stir together bouillon granules, thyme, oregano, rosemary, black pepper, and garlic powder.
2. In two pint canning jars or other glass jars layer ingredients in the following order: herb mixture, pasta, onion, tomatoes, sweet pepper, and mushrooms. Tap jars gently on towel-lined counter to settle each layer before adding the next. Seal jars. Attach directions for making Italian Meatball Soup.

To make Italian Meatball Soup: Remove mushrooms and place in a small bowl. Add enough boiling water to cover; let stand for 20 minutes. Remove mushrooms with a slotted spoon. Rinse and chop mushrooms. Empty the remaining contents of the jar into a 4-quart Dutch oven. Stir in 8 cups water and chopped mushrooms. Bring to boiling; reduce heat. Simmer, covered, for 8 minutes. Add one 12-ounce package (12 meatballs) frozen cooked Italian-flavor turkey meatballs, thawed, and 3 cups coarsely chopped kale. Return to boiling; reduce heat. Simmer, uncovered, for 2 to 3 minutes or until pasta is tender and meatballs are heated through. Makes 6 (1½-cup) servings.

Make a Scene

The focal point of this gift is a snowman trim accompanied by a tiny bottlebrush tree. To lend interest to the jar lid, wrap it with jute, hot-gluing in place. To dress up the baguette, wrap it with a clean bread cloth, then tie snuggly with jute. Slip the baguette into a cellophane bag to keep it fresh.

PASTA-HERB SOU
MIX and SAGE-O
BAGUETTES

ITALIAN MEATBALL SOUP
recipe on page 129

Sage-Olive Baguettes

WHAT YOU NEED

3½ to 4 cups bread flour or unbleached all-purpose flour
1 package active dry yeast
¾ teaspoon salt
1¼ cups warm water (120°F to 130°F)
½ cup coarsely chopped, pitted Kalamata olives
2 to 3 tablespoons snipped fresh sage or 2 to 3 teaspoons dried sage, crushed
1 egg white, lightly beaten
1 tablespoon water

WHAT YOU DO

1. In a large mixing bowl stir together 1 cup of the flour, the yeast, and salt. Add the 1¼ cups warm water. Beat with an electric mixer on low to medium speed for 30 seconds, scraping sides of bowl constantly. Beat on high speed for 3 minutes. Stir in the olives and sage. Using a wooden spoon, stir in as much of the remaining flour as you can.
2. Turn dough out onto a lightly floured surface. Knead in enough remaining flour to make a stiff dough that is smooth and elastic (8 to 10 minutes). Shape dough into a ball. Place in a lightly greased bowl, turning once to grease surface of dough. Cover; let rise in a warm place until double in size (about 1 hour).
3. Punch dough down. Turn dough out onto a lightly floured surface. Divide in half; shape into balls. Cover; let rest for 10 minutes. Meanwhile, lightly grease two baking sheets or two baguette pans; sprinkle lightly with flour. Set aside.
4. Roll each half of dough into a 14×5-inch rectangle. Starting from long sides, tightly roll up rectangles. Pinch seams to seal and slightly pull to taper ends. Place loaves, seam sides down, on prepared baking sheets. In a small bowl stir together egg white and the 1 tablespoon water; brush some on loaves. Let rise until nearly double in size (35 to 45 minutes).
5. Preheat oven to 375°F. Using a sharp knife, make three or four ¼-inch-deep diagonal cuts across each loaf top. Bake for 20 minutes. Brush again with egg white mixture. Bake for 10 to 15 minutes more or until bread sounds hollow when lightly tapped. Immediately transfer bread to wire racks to cool. Makes 2 loaves.

BARLEY SOUP MIX

BRANDY-SOAKED CURRANT, THYME, AND PARMESAN SCONES
recipe on page 133

Barley Soup Mix

WHAT YOU NEED

½ cup dried green or brown lentils
½ cup instant chicken bouillon granules
1 teaspoon dried basil, crushed
½ teaspoon dried oregano, crushed
½ teaspoon dried rosemary, crushed
½ teaspoon ground black pepper
¼ teaspoon garlic powder
1 cup regular pearl barley
⅓ cup dried minced onion
¾ cup chopped dried mushrooms
½ cup snipped dried tomatoes

WHAT YOU DO

1. Rinse lentils. Spread lentils in a single layer on paper towels; let stand for 8 to 24 hours or until completely dry.
2. In a small bowl stir together chicken bouillon granules, basil, oregano, rosemary, pepper, and garlic powder. In each of two 1-pint glass jars layer in the following order: half the lentils, half the pearl barley, half the dried minced onion, half the dried mushrooms, half the chicken bouillon mixture, and half of the dried tomatoes. Tap jar gently on towel-lined counter to settle each layer before adding the next; seal. Attach directions to make Barley Soup.
To make Barley Soup: Empty the contents of 1 jar into a Dutch oven. Stir in 8½ cups water, 1½ cups chopped cooked chicken (about 8 ounces), and 3 medium carrots, sliced (1½ cups). Bring to boiling; reduce heat. Cover and simmer for 35 to 40 minutes or until barley is tender. Makes 6 main-dish servings.

Simply Done

Present this gift of scones and soup in a large shallow basket lined with a cloth napkin. Tie a tag with a holiday message around the neck of the jar using twine. Slip the entire arrangement into a large cellophane gift bag to keep scones fresh.

ACCORDION CHEESE BREAD

Cool Trim

A laser-cut wood ornament tied to a jar handle is an added gift. For bread, wrap with a strip of parchment paper and a ribbon.

SPICY MIXED BEAN SOUP WITH CORN CHIPS

Brandy-Soaked Currant, Thyme, and Parmesan Scones

WHAT YOU NEED

½ cup dried currants
¼ cup brandy or apple juice
1¾ cups all-purpose flour
¾ cup finely shredded Parmigiano-Reggiano cheese (3 ounces)
1 tablespoon baking powder
1 tablespoon sugar
1 tablespoon snipped fresh thyme
1 teaspoon freshly ground black pepper
½ teaspoon salt
¼ cup cold butter, cut up
⅔ cup whipping cream
1 egg
1 tablespoon water
Snipped fresh thyme (optional)

WHAT YOU DO

1. Line a baking sheet with parchment paper; set aside.
2. In a small saucepan combine currants and brandy. Heat over medium heat just until warm; remove from heat. Cover and let stand for 15 minutes. Drain.
3. In a food processor* combine flour, ½ cup of the cheese, the baking powder, sugar, thyme, pepper, and salt; cover and pulse with several on/off turns to combine. Sprinkle butter pieces over flour mixture; cover and pulse with several on/off turns until mixture resembles coarse crumbs. Add drained currants; cover and pulse with several on/off turns to combine. With the motor running, slowly add whipping cream through the feed tube, processing just until combined.
4. Turn dough out onto a lightly floured surface. Knead dough by folding and gently pressing it for 10 to 12 strokes or just until dough holds together. Pat or lightly roll dough into an 8-inch circle about ¾ inch thick. In a small bowl whisk together egg and the water; brush over dough circle. Sprinkle with the remaining ¼ cup cheese and, if desired, additional snipped fresh thyme. Using a pizza cutter or floured sharp knife, cut circle into 8 wedges. Cover and chill for 30 minutes up to overnight.
5. Preheat oven to 375°F. Bake about 20 minutes or until scones are golden. Remove scones from baking sheet; serve warm or cool completely. Place cooled scones in bag; close bag. Attach directions for reheating scones.** Makes 8 scones.
***Tip:** If you don't have a food processor, combine flour mixture in a large bowl. Using a pastry blender, cut in butter until mixture resembles coarse crumbs. Stir in currants. Make a well in center of flour mixture. Add whipping cream all at once to flour mixture. Using a fork, stir just until moistened. Continue as directed.
****To reheat scones:** Wrap scones in foil. Reheat in a 350°F oven for 12 to 15 minutes or until heated through.

Spicy Mixed Bean Soup with Corn Chips

WHAT YOU NEED

1½ cups dehydrated mixed vegetables
1 ounce dried tomatoes (not oil-packed) (¼ cup)
2 tablespoons instant chicken bouillon granules
1 tablespoon dried minced onion
1 tablespoon dried parsley
1 to 2 teaspoons Mexican, fajita, Jamaican jerk, or Cajun seasoning
¾ teaspoon garlic powder
½ to ¾ teaspoon ground chipotle chile pepper, cayenne pepper, or ground black pepper
2 bay leaves
½ cup dried pinto beans
½ cup dried red kidney or black beans or dried cranberry beans
½ cup dried navy beans or dried Great Northern beans
Shredded sharp cheddar cheese (optional)
Corn chips

WHAT YOU DO

For seasoning mix: In a small plastic bag combine dehydrated mixed vegetables, tomatoes, bouillon granules, dried onion, parsley, Mexican seasoning, garlic powder, chipotle chile pepper, and bay leaves. Seal; set aside.
For soup mix: Layer in a 1-quart glass jar or 32-ounce canister or container with a tight-fitting lid the following ingredients one at a time in this order: pinto beans, kidney beans, and navy beans. Tap jar gently on towel-lined counter to settle each layer before adding the next. Place bag of seasoning mix in jar. Cover the jar. Attach directions for making Spicy Mixed Bean Soup with Corn Chips.
To make Spicy Mixed Bean Soup with Corn Chips: Remove seasoning mix; set aside. Rinse beans. In a large saucepan combine beans and 4 cups water. Bring to boiling; reduce heat. Simmer, uncovered, for 2 minutes. Remove from heat. Cover; let stand for 1 hour. (Or place beans in water in pan. Cover; let soak in a cool place overnight.) Drain and rinse beans. In the same saucepan combine beans, 6 cups fresh water, and seasoning mix. Bring to boiling; reduce heat. Simmer, covered, for 1¼ to 1½ hours or until beans are tender. Discard bay leaves. Top with shredded cheddar cheese and serve with corn chips. Makes 6 servings.
Slow Cooker Directions: Rinse beans. Place in a large saucepan or Dutch oven. Add 4 cups cold water to cover. Bring to boiling; reduce heat. Simmer, uncovered, 10 minutes. Remove from heat. Cover; let stand 1 hour. Rinse and drain beans. Transfer beans to a 3½- or 4-quart slow cooker. Add 6 cups fresh water and seasoning mix. Cover and cook on low-heat setting for 8 to 10 hours or on high-heat setting for 4 to 5 hours. Discard bay leaves. Top with shredded cheddar cheese and serve with corn chips.

Accordion Cheese Bread

WHAT YOU NEED

1¼ cups milk
⅓ cup butter
⅓ cup sugar
1 teaspoon salt
1 package active dry yeast
1 egg
4 to 4¼ cups all-purpose flour
¼ cup butter, melted
1 tablespoon Dijon-style mustard
¼ teaspoon bottled hot pepper sauce
1 cup finely shredded sharp cheddar cheese (4 ounces)
½ cup finely chopped green onions (4)

WHAT YOU DO

1. In a medium saucepan combine the milk, butter, sugar, and salt. Heat over low heat until warm (105°F to 115°F). Remove from heat. Stir in yeast until dissolved. In a large mixing bowl beat the egg with a fork. Add the milk mixture and 1½ cups of the flour. Beat with an electric mixer on low speed for 1 minute, scraping sides of bowl constantly.
2. Using a wooden spoon, stir in enough of the remaining flour to make a soft

CHILE-CHEDDAR CASSEROLE BREAD

MEXICAN THREE-BEAN CHILI MIX

dough that just starts to pull away from the sides of the bowl (dough will be slightly sticky). Transfer dough to a large lightly greased bowl. Cover; let rise in a warm place until nearly double in size (1 to 1½ hours).

3. Punch dough down. Turn dough out onto a lightly floured surface. Divide dough in half. Cover; let rest for 10 minutes. Meanwhile, lightly grease two 8×4×2-inch loaf pans. In a small bowl stir together the melted butter, mustard, and hot pepper sauce.

4. On a lightly floured surface roll one dough half into a 20×12-inch rectangle. Brush with half the butter mixture. Sprinkle evenly with half the cheese and onions. Cut the dough crosswise into 6 equal strips. Stack the strips. Cut the stacked strips crosswise into 6 equal pieces. Arrange the stacked pieces next to each other, cut sides up, in loaf pan.* Repeat with remaining dough, butter mixture, cheese, and onions in second loaf pan. Sprinkle any spilled cheese and onions on top and drizzle with any remaining butter mixture. Cover; let rise in a warm place for 30 minutes.

5. Preheat oven to 350°F. Bake for 40 minutes, covering loaves with foil the last 15 minutes of baking to prevent overbrowning. Cool in pans on a wire rack. Remove loaves from pans. Wrap as directed below. Attach directions for reheating loaves.** Makes 2 loaves.

***Test Kitchen Tip:** To easily transfer stacked dough into the pan, tip pan up on its short side and use a spatula to transfer the dough squares.

****To reheat bread:** Wrap loaf in foil. Place in a 350°F oven 30 minutes or until heated through. Pull bread apart to serve.

To make ahead: Prepare as directed through Step 2. Cover and refrigerate dough overnight. Continue as directed.

Western Wear

A clean red or green bandana sets the theme for this delicious duo. Drape it in a basket or wooden bowl to cushion pieces of bread. For soup, place mix in a jar and tie with chunky jute. Thread large wooden beads on each tail and hot-glue a jingle bell to each end to secure. For lid, hot-glue a pinecone and artificial greenery to the center.

Mexican Three-Bean Chili Mix

WHAT YOU NEED

- 2 pounds dried black beans
- 2 pounds dried pinto beans
- 2 pounds dried Great Northern beans
- ¾ cup dried minced onion
- ¾ cup dried green sweet pepper
- ¾ cup chili powder
- ½ cup packed brown sugar
- 1 3-ounce package dried tomatoes (not oil-packed), cut into thin strips
- 3 tablespoons dried oregano, crushed
- 3 tablespoons ground cumin
- 2 tablespoons unsweetened cocoa powder
- 2 tablespoons garlic salt
- 1 tablespoon ground black pepper

WHAT YOU DO

In an extra-large bowl stir together black, pinto, and Great Northern beans. Divide beans among eight glass jars (1⅔ cups per jar); set aside. In a medium bowl stir together dried onion, dried sweet pepper, chili powder, brown sugar, dried tomatoes, oregano, cumin, cocoa powder, garlic salt, and black pepper. Divide mixture among eight small plastic bags; seal bags. Place seasoning mix bags on top of beans; seal jars. Attach directions for making Mexican Three-Bean Chili.

To make Mexican Three-Bean Chili: Rinse beans. In a 6- to 8-quart Dutch oven combine beans and 8 cups water. Bring to boiling; reduce heat. Simmer, uncovered, for 2 minutes. Remove from heat. Cover and let stand for 1 hour. (Or place beans and water in Dutch oven. Cover and let soak in a cool place for 6 to 8 hours or overnight.) Drain and rinse beans. In the same Dutch oven combine beans, two 14.5-ounce cans undrained diced tomatoes; one 14.5-ounce can beef broth; one 12-ounce can beer, nonalcoholic beer, or one 14-ounce can beef broth; one 8-ounce can tomato sauce; and one bag seasoning mix. Stir in 2 cups water. Bring to boiling; reduce heat. Cover and simmer about 2 hours or until beans are tender, stirring occasionally. If desired, serve with sour cream, shredded Mexican cheese blend, and/or sliced green onions. Makes 6 servings.

Chile-Cheddar Casserole Bread

WHAT YOU NEED

- ¼ cup warm hot-style vegetable juice (105°F to 115°F)
- 1 package active dry yeast
- 1 cup sour cream
- ¼ cup finely chopped onion
- 2 eggs
- 2 tablespoons sugar
- 1 teaspoon salt
- ½ teaspoon ancho chile powder
- 2½ cups all-purpose flour
- 1⅓ cups finely shredded sharp cheddar cheese (about 5 ounces)
- 1 4-ounce can fire-roasted diced green chiles, undrained
- Sliced green onions (optional)

WHAT YOU DO

1. In a large mixing bowl combine vegetable juice and yeast; let stand until mixture is foamy. Add sour cream, onion, eggs, sugar, salt, ancho chile powder, and 1 cup of the flour. Beat with an electric mixer on medium speed for 2 minutes. Using a wooden spoon, stir in the remaining 1½ cups flour, 1 cup of the cheese, and the green chiles until a soft, sticky dough forms.

2. Transfer dough to a greased 2-quart oval or rectangular baking dish. Cover; let rise in a warm place until double in size (1 to 1½ hours).

3. Preheat oven to 350°F. Bake for 40 minutes; remove from oven and sprinkle with remaining cheese. Return to oven; bake for 5 minutes more. Cool in dish on a wire rack for 10 minutes. Remove bread from dish. Cool on wire rack for 20 minutes. Makes 8 servings.

In a Twinkling Jingle Bells

A Touch of Gold

Whether gently poured into a glass ornament, sprinkled on the table, or topping mini trees, these shiny bells add a festive touch to holiday tablescapes. Place a large one in the center of the place setting to create a focal point.

Tied and True

A ring of bells hugs cloth napkins. Cut an 8-inch length of medium-weight wire. Thread 6 inches with small silver bells. Use pliers to twist wire ends together near bells; clip off excess wire. Thread three large bells on narrow ribbon; tie to ring, covering twisted ends.

Jingle Wreath

Neutral ribbons and jingle bells lend a shabby-chic look to a natural wreath. Make a pretty bow using a combination of wide and narrow ribbons; notch ribbon ends for a finished appearance. Wire the bow to the wreath. Thread a pair of large jingle bells onto a length of wire and snug them tight to the center of the bow; twist the ends together on the back side of the wreath.

Musical Message

Whether an invitation, holiday greeting, or thank-you note, these dimensional cards make fond impressions. Create a layered card from cardstock as shown, leaving a white rectangle (approximately 4×3 inches) in the center. Hot-glue six large and three small jingle bells, tree-style, on the front as shown. To keep trims intact, this beauty deserves hand delivery.

Bell of the Ball

When it's time to adorn the table for the holidays, this easy accompaniment does the trick. Hot-glue tinsel trim to the edge of a plate charger. For a lively focal point, add a sheer ribbon bow with a decorative jingle bell glued to the center. Tone-on-tone color sets off the silver bell accent. To clean, wipe charger with a wet cloth; don't immerse in water.

kids

LITTLE HANDS BIG IMAGINATIONS

ENCOURAGE

Little ones to get creative, too, with fun projects for them to stitch, paint, decoupage, stamp, and more.

Party-Time Table

Pink and green put kid-style spin on traditional holiday hues. To set a festive mood, surround each place setting with oodles of curling ribbon.

Polka-Dot Plates

The easy-to-make tree motif grabs attention on this plate. Small polka dots create the festive confetti border.

WHAT YOU NEED

Clear glass plate
Paper punch
Paper in red, pink, light green, and medium green
1-inch-wide paintbrush
Decoupage medium
¾-inch round punch
White tissue paper
Silver chenille stem
Fingernail polish bottle, dowel, or other round shape approximately ½ inch in diameter
Hot-glue gun and glue sticks

WHAT YOU DO

1. Use the paper punch to make dozens of dots from each color of paper. Working in small areas at a time, brush the rim of the back side of the plate with decoupage medium as shown in Photo A.
2. While decoupage medium is wet, sprinkle on a few punched dots, as shown in Photo B. For easy placement, dot a toothpick or the brush into a tiny amount of glue and use it to pick up and place each dot.
3. Brush a coat of decoupage medium over the dot group as shown in Photo C. Continue adding dots around the entire rim of the plate to cover uniformly.
4. Brush the center of the plate with decoupage medium. Punch out 6 large dots from dark green paper. While decoupage medium is wet, place the large dots in a triangular tree shape with a small pink dot on the top for a star and four red dots for the trunk. Reapply decoupage medium as needed as shown in Photo D to keep area wet so all pieces stick.
5. Crinkle a sheet of tissue paper, then carefully flatten. Brush the back of the plate with decoupage medium. Immediately press tissue paper over the wet decoupage medium as shown in Photo E.
6. Trim away excess tissue paper as shown in Photo F.
7. Use a fingernail polish bottle to shape several chenille stems into scallops as shown in Photo G.
8. Working in small sections at a time, hot-glue scalloped chenille around the plate edge, gluing to the backside as shown in Photo H.
9. Hot-glue chenille stems around the plate edge as shown in Photo I, using as many as needed to cover the edge.
10. To wash plates, do not soak. Wash the plate front with a soapy cloth, then rinse off. Immediately dry with a towel.

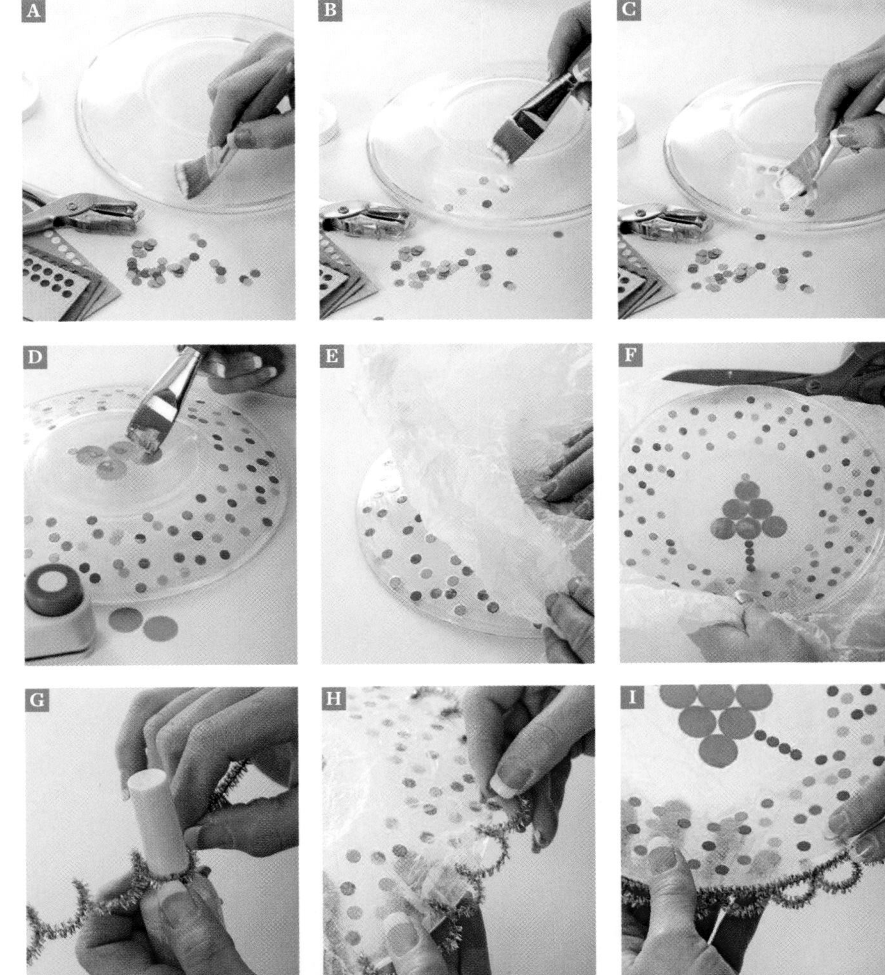

Treat Take-Home

Treat party guests with sweets to enjoy later. To make a handle for a small baby food jar, use two chenille stems. With stems aligned, twist stems together 2 inches from one end. Insert the jar between the long stem ends, then twist the stem tails to secure to jar. Twist the chenille stem ends together for a handle, straightening the tail ends as shown. Make a loop from wire-edge ribbon and hot-glue to handle to resemble a leaf. Glue on buttons and a flowing length of ribbon for the extra aha.

Service with Style

Jars can hold anything from candy canes to breadsticks for a party. Decorate the serving pieces with ribbon, buttons, and chenille stems. Hot-glue a ribbon around the jar. Edge the top and bottom with chenille stems, twisting the ends to secure. Lace tiny buttons with chenille stem, twist the ends together on the back, and cut short. Hot-glue a tiny button on a larger button and glue to ribbon as shown. Hot-glue a short length of chenille stem around button edges.

First Name Basis

Mark each guest's spot with initialed place cards. Place approximately 2-inch letters on 2½-inch squares of cardstock. Glue to the front of a 2¾-inch square folded card. Hot-glue a small ribbon bow to the upper left corner. Cut and shape chenille stem and glue on to accent the letter as shown.

Bottle Beauty

Nudge a glass of milk into a special party beverage by bottling it up stylishly. Hot-glue a wide band of ribbon around each short clean recycled bottle. Then add narrow ribbon bows with jingle bell centers to the front. Drop in a couple of printed straws, and they're ready to pour in ice-cold milk.

Red and White Delights

Candy-cane colors set the stage for jolly decorations that are glued, folded, painted, and sewn.

Mini Pom-Pom Wreath Ornament

Kids will help assemble these miniature Christmas ornaments. Add a few to a tree or string a garland full to dress up a mantel. Choose tinsel pom-poms in assorted sizes. Cover a small plastic-foam wreath with ⅛-inch-wide ribbon; secure ends with short pins. Make a hanging loop with ¼-inch-wide ribbon. Hot-glue pom-poms to the ribbon-covered wreath, filling in gaps with tiny pom-poms.

Red Paper Christmas Tree

This mini Christmas tree made from folded paper is a chic accent for holiday dessert buffets. To make, use two pieces of 12-inch squares of red cardstock. Cut two 2½×12-inch strips. Cut two 12-inch strips ⅛ inch narrower than the first strips, then cut two 12-inch strips ⅛ inch narrower than the second strips. Cut two progressively narrower strips until all cardstock is trimmed. Lay a strip on a scoring board; score ½-inch crosswise lines on all strips.

Punch one long edge of each strip with a scallop-edge punch. Accordion-fold the strips on scored lines. Use clear-drying glue to adhere the short edges of two strips together to shape a medallion. Squeeze the medallion together to close the opening in the center, then secure with hot glue. Repeat for all strips.

To make small medallions for the top third of the tree, shorten the strips before joining pairs. Hot-glue folded medallions together to shape the tree, starting with the largest medallion at the bottom and ending with the smallest medallion at the top. Hot-glue a ball ornament to the top of the tree.

Pretty White Felt Ornaments

Create a bunch of these pretty ornaments to use as gift toppers, on the tree, or to trim a wreath.

WHAT YOU NEED

9×12-inch ivory felt
Moss green felt scrap
Water-soluble marking pen
Straight pins
Pinking shears
Large-eye needle
Embroidery floss in red, light green, and ivory
Polyester fiberfill
Jingle bell

WHAT YOU DO

1. Trace the patterns, pages 156–157, onto white paper; cut out. Trace two bells, two wreaths, and two trees onto ivory felt; cut approximately ½ inch outside traced lines. Trace four leaves onto green felt; cut out.
2. Tape ornament patterns to a light box. Tape one ivory felt piece over each pattern and trace dots and lines for ornament front.
3. Pin together each set of pieces, wrong sides together. Cut along edges using pinking shears. Use straight-edge scissors to cut the center of the wreath. Remove traced outlines with a damp paper towel; unpin the pieces.
4. Stitch a French knot (see stitches on page 155) with four strands of red embroidery floss at each dot. Straight-stitch the star on the bell ornament with four strands of red floss.
5. Pin each embroidered ornament front to its matching back, wrong sides together. Whipstitch around inner circle of wreath using ivory floss.
6. Use running stitches and red or ivory floss to sew together each ornament just inside pinked edges, leaving a 1½-inch opening along one edge.
7. Stuff each ornament with polyester fiberfill; stitch opening closed.
8. Stitch together leaf pieces in pairs, using a running stitch and light green floss. Stitch leaves to top of wreath.
9. Using six strands of red floss, stitch through the top of each ornament; trim floss to desired length for hanging loop. Tie floss ends in a knot. Stitch a jingle bell to bottom of bell ornament using ivory floss.

Jingle Bell Flower Ornament

Upcycle an egg carton to create jingle bell roses for your tree. Cut off the lid of a cardboard egg carton, then cut around each individual egg cup using the photo for reference. Cut leaf shapes from the flat cardboard pieces. Paint each egg cup red; paint leaves green. Use a yarn needle to poke a hole through the center of each egg cup and one end of each leaf. Thread needle with yarn and string on three leaves. Poke needle through egg cup, thread on a jingle bell, and poke needle back through cup. Add three more leaves to the yarn and trim to desired length. Knot ends for hanging loop.

Wool Yarn Bird Ornament

This pretty bird ornament perches on a tree. Use pom-pom makers and red wool yarn to make one large and one extra-large dense pom-pom; tie each with waxed twine. Trim large pom-pom with sharp scissors to shape head; create a flat area on bottom of head. Shape extra-large pom-pom for body, trimming a concave area in back and sides flat. Shape a pointed end for tail, leaving tail yarns uneven. Trim a flat area at the top of body; glue pom-poms together. Glue black beads to head for eyes and glue two tiny peach felt triangles for beak. Tie a 12-inch length of white satin ribbon around the neck; tie in a bow. Glue a silk flower to the head. Adhere an ornament clip to the bottom of the bird.

In a Twinkling
It's a Wrap

Snow Fellas
Wrap gifts with character. Cover gift box with plain colored paper. Draw snowmen and simple snowflakes using a marking pen. Color in the design using colored pencils.

Star Struck
Who would guess this elegant wrap is made using a potato! With an adult's help, cut a potato in half. Press a star-shape cookie cutter into the cut side of the potato and carefully cut away the edges to make a stamp. Dip the star shape into acrylic paint, then dab onto paper to cover randomly.

Subtle Stripes

To make pretty striped paper, cover a work surface with newspaper. Cut solid wrapping paper to the desired size. Cut $1\frac{1}{2}$-inch strips of newspaper and lay over wrapping paper about 2 inches apart. To make speckled stripes, dip a toothbrush into acrylic paint and press thumb across bristles to fleck paint onto paper until areas between strips are speckled; let dry and remove strips. Dip a pencil eraser into paint and dot in a row inside the unpainted stripes; let dry.

Lotsa Circles

Dots and circles, big and small, combine to make this festive wrap. Use items such as paper towel tubes, dowels, pencil erasers, cans, and other circles to make the design. For each size, place acrylic paint on a plate and dip the item into the paint; press onto paper and let dry. Continue the process with a new color and item to make a wide stripe of overlapping circles.

Jingle Jangle Wreath

Here's a great wrap for little ones. Put a small amount of two shades of acrylic green paint onto a paper plate. Press thumb into paint and dab onto paper in a wreath shape. Let dry. Hot-glue jingle bells in sets of three and a ribbon bow to the wreath.

Patterns

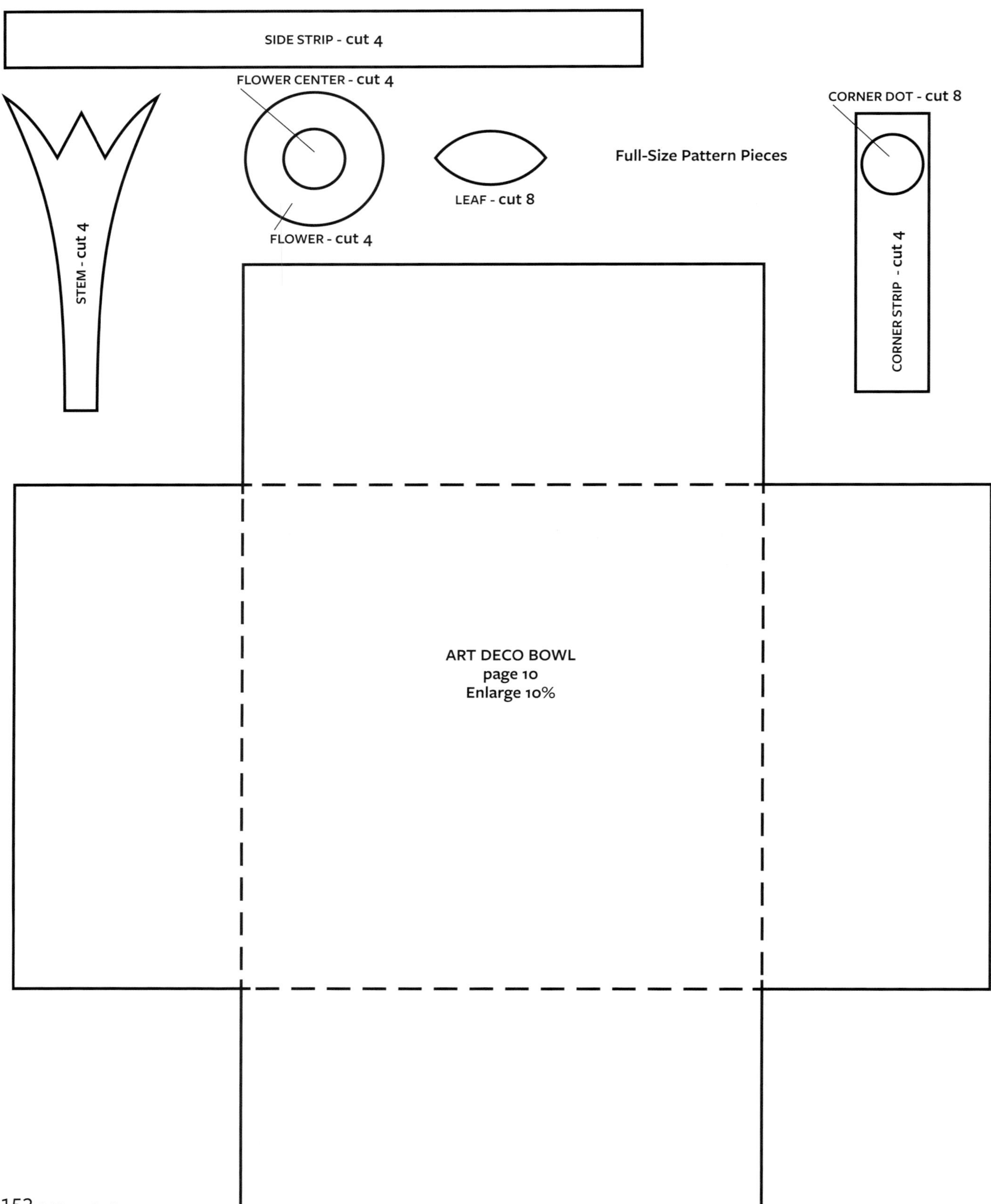

SIDE STRIP - cut 4
FLOWER CENTER - cut 4
CORNER DOT - cut 8
STEM - cut 4
LEAF - cut 8
Full-Size Pattern Pieces
FLOWER - cut 4
CORNER STRIP - cut 4
ART DECO BOWL
page 10
Enlarge 10%

ARTFUL COASTERS
page 9
Full-Size Patterns

FALLING LEAVES MAT
page 8
Full-Size Patterns

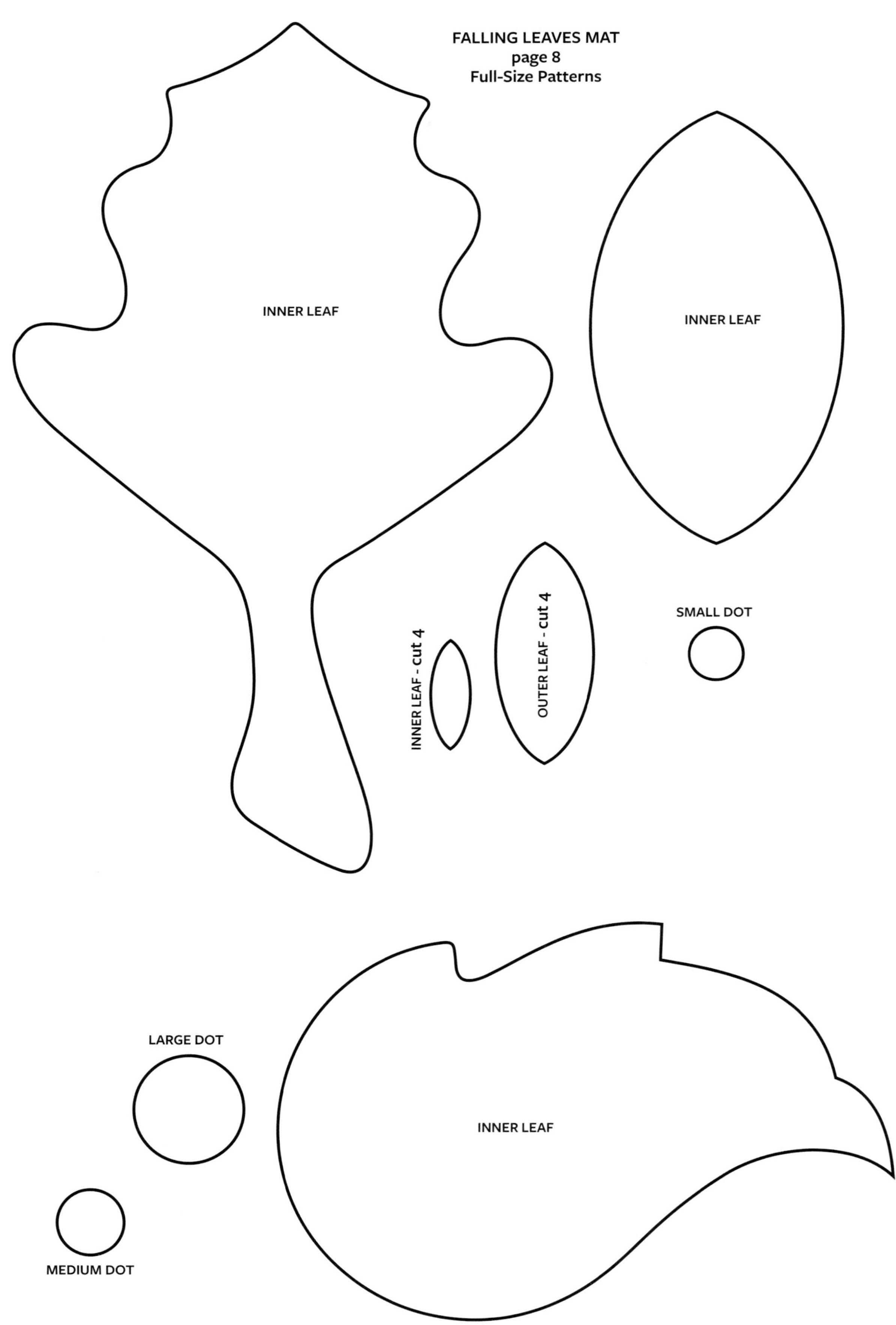

FELTED FEATHERED FRIENDS
page 75
Full-Size Patterns

BIRD HEAD

BIRD BODY

BEAK

WING

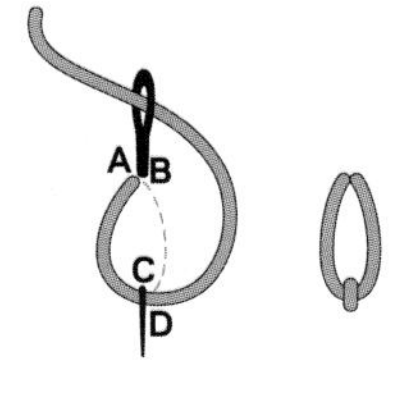

LAZY DAISY STITCH

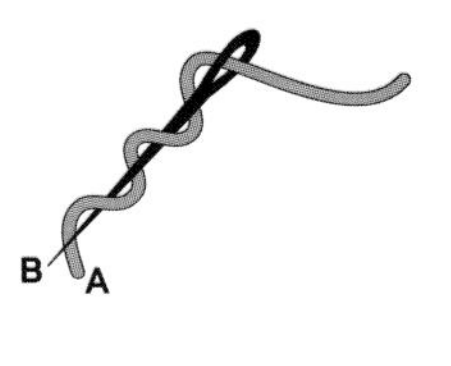

FRENCH KNOT

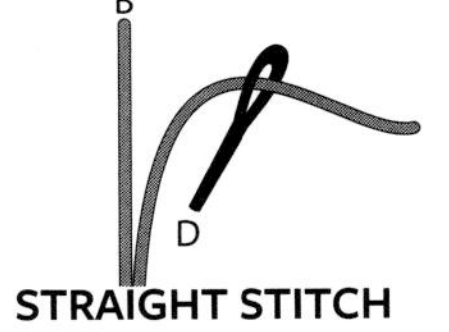

STRAIGHT STITCH

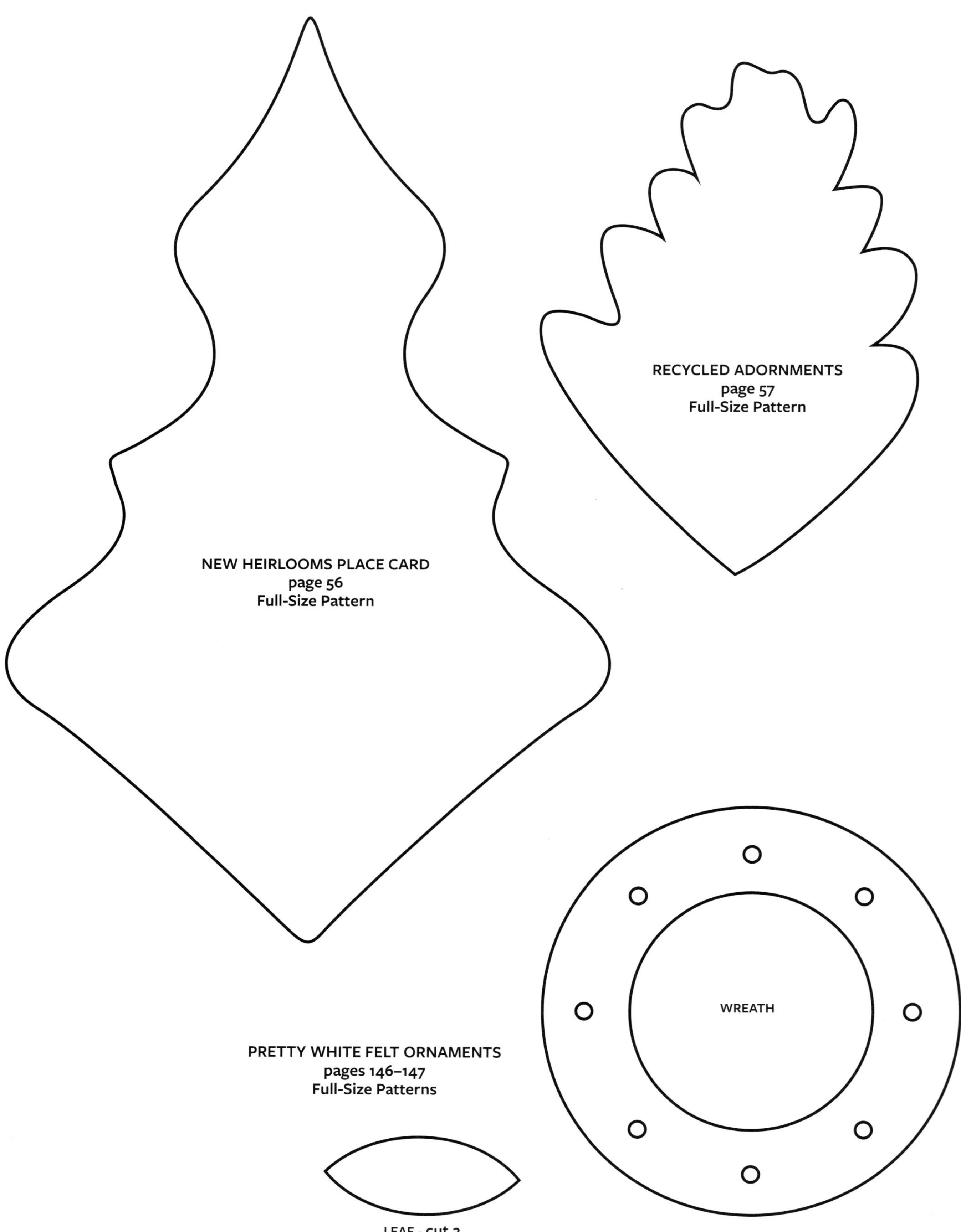
RECYCLED ADORNMENTS
page 57
Full-Size Pattern
NEW HEIRLOOMS PLACE CARD
page 56
Full-Size Pattern
WREATH
PRETTY WHITE FELT ORNAMENTS
pages 146–147
Full-Size Patterns
LEAF - cut 2

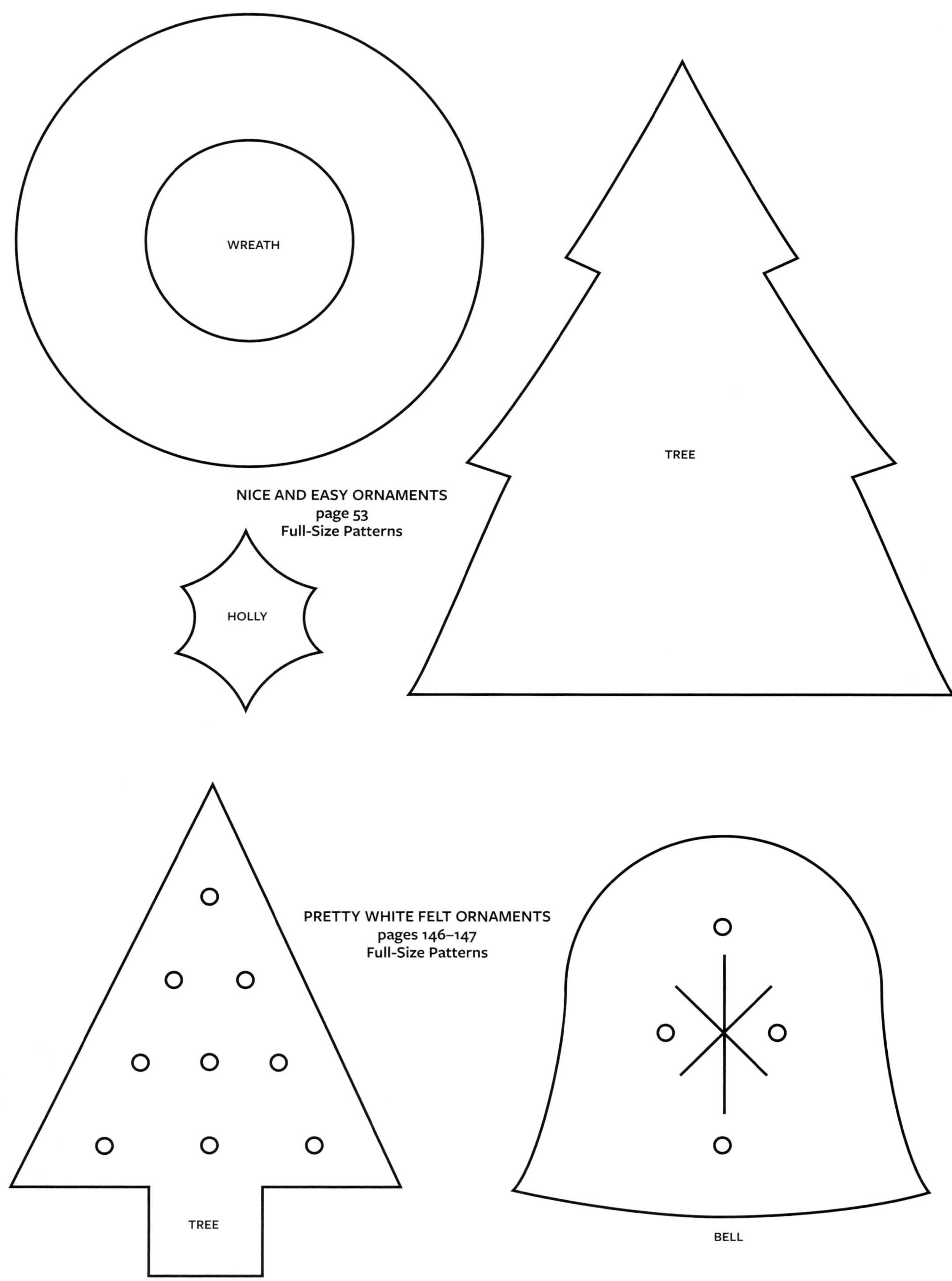
WREATH
TREE
NICE AND EASY ORNAMENTS
page 53
Full-Size Patterns
HOLLY
PRETTY WHITE FELT ORNAMENTS
pages 146–147
Full-Size Patterns
TREE
BELL

SCENIC VIEW
pages 52–53
Full-Size Patterns

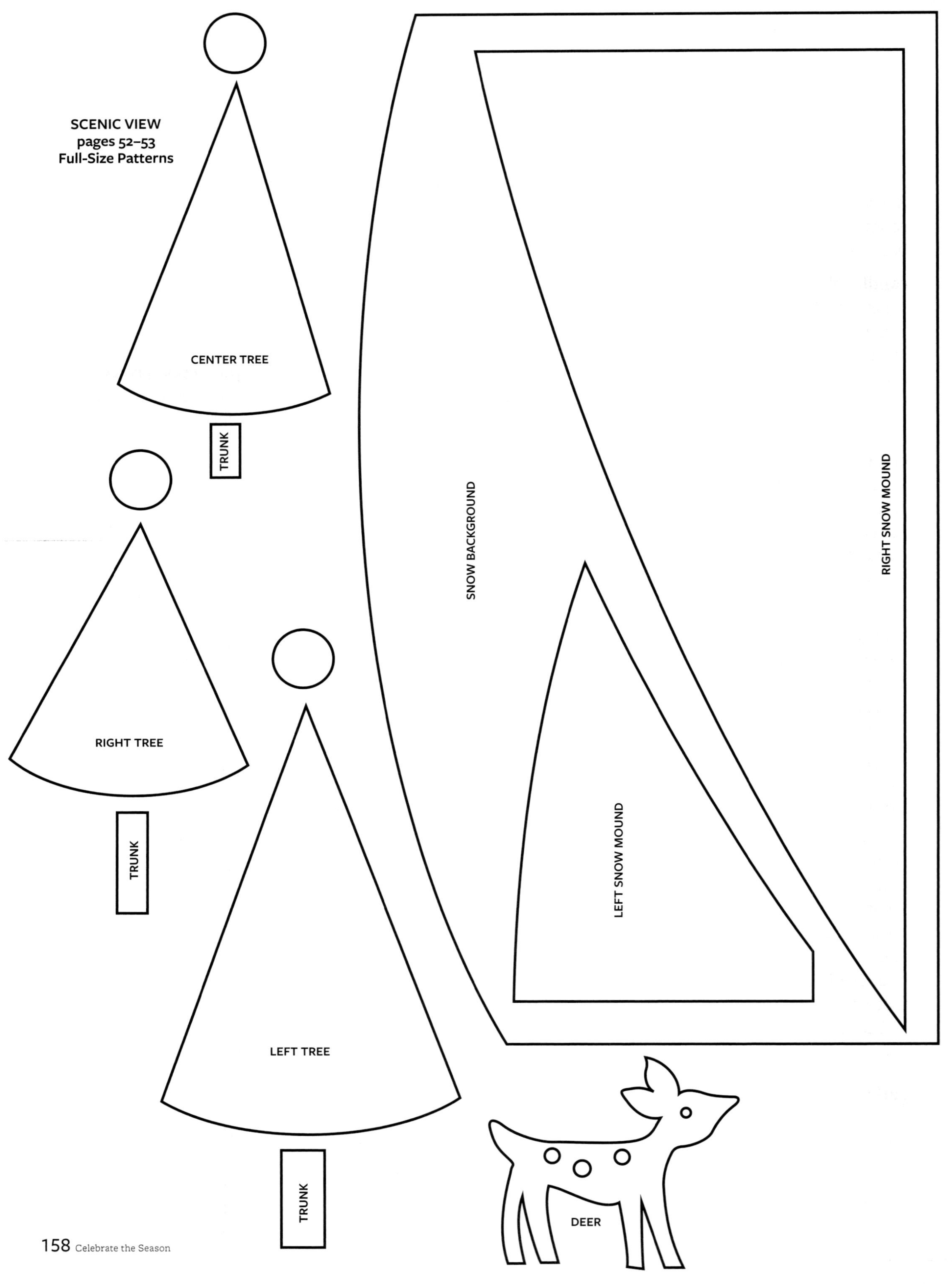

Index

CRAFTS AND DECORATING

index *continued*

CREDITS

Photo Styling
Sue Banker
Cathy Brett

Photography
Marty Baldwin
Jay Wilde